*Morrison, John Harrison*

# History of New York ship yards

*Inktank publishing*

*Morrison, John Harrison*

**History of New York ship yards**

*Inktank publishing, 2018*

*www.inktank-publishing.com*

*ISBN/EAN: 9783747775271*

# HISTORY

OF

# New York Ship Yards

BY

JOHN H. MORRISON

AUTHOR
"HISTORY OF AMERICAN STEAM NAVIGATION"

PRESS OF
WM. F. SAMETZ & CO.
NEW YORK

# CONTENTS.

# ILLUSTRATIONS.

# PREFACE.

HE development of shipbuilding in New York prior to the separation of the colony from the Mother Country, both under the Dutch as well as the English occupation, was of a very uncertain character, mainly for the reason that for the greater portion of the period the commerce carried on with foreign countries was with vessels owned abroad, and it was only toward the latter days of the colony that vessels were constructed in this city for trading coastwise for any distance, and to the West Indies. There were vessels built for near-by trade, but they were comparatively small in dimensions and number. For the reason that our forefathers were not given to the habit of recording any advancement made in industrial pursuits in this country, it is impossible to cover the subject but in a general manner during the Colonial period.

It was not until after the treaty of peace with Great Britain in September, 1783, that there are any records of shipbuilding in the City of New York. In fact, while the several States still retained their separate governments, to the formation of the Union of States in 1789, there is no record to be found in this city. So there is no official record of vessels built in this city prior to President Washington's administration, and even for a few years later there are some of the official papers of New York built vessels, that have been for many years among the missing.

The industry now began to show much activity compared to its former condition, and the restless energy of the American mechanic began to assert itself in its first stage of freedom from foreign control, and while the progress in the "art of shipbuilding" was very small indeed, it was not until after the monopoly of steam navigation on our rivers was removed in 1824 that we see the vast improvements that took place in shipbuilding in this city. From this period to its final decline about forty years later, it was a rapid development with the large growth of the city and its many industries.

In the first stage of this expansion of shipbuilding, the skilled mechanic began the agitation for the relief from his long hours of labor, and in a few years he was successful, and through the several changes in the methods of construction, and the use of better tools, work was turned out more rapidly and better than before. Then came the building of Ocean and Coastwise Steamships, and later the far-famed Clipper ships, for which New York City was so widely noted, and justly so. This lasted for a few years; and then several surrounding conditions, all affecting the shipbuilding industry of the city, more or less, had the effect to stop the making of new contracts for vessels, and to close up some of the local shipyards. The progress in the industry at New York was followed during the whole period at all the shipbuilding centers on the Atlantic Coast, but this city was the most unfortunate in losing its hold upon this business so soon after the close of the conflict between the States in 1865. The State of Maine was the exception, for wooden shipbuilding was largely carried on there till very recent date.

Had the builders and owners of vessel property at that day the foresight to have seen that the day of the wooden hull vessel had passed, generally, they would have been saved many anxious days waiting for its return to prosperity. Some no doubt did see it, and retired from business before it was too late, while others remained to the last. The prosperous days of the wooden hull shipyards had passed, the iron hull shipyards took their business, and the former passed into history. The old Mechanics Bell and the Balance Dry Dock are about the only material evidences we have left of the industry. The American wooden-hull shipbuilder was undoubtedly a credit to the nation in his day.

# CHAPTER I.

## COLONIAL PERIOD.

### DURING DUTCH AND ENGLISH OCCUPATION OF NEW YORK CITY.

HE Atlantic coast being well fitted for shipbuilding by the abundance of its timber, vessels have been constructed at several points on its northern and eastern shores from the first actual settlement of the country by Europeans. That which made it almost a work of necessity was the fact that the early colonists were located along the immediate coast, and were forced at first to build the Indian canoe to obtain the fish for a food product for their own use; but a few years later they built small sail vessels that gave them a wider range in their fishing operations than with a canoe.

The earliest record we have of the construction of a vessel in this country, other than small fishing boats, is of one built by colonists sent to the coast of Maine by some merchants of London in 1607, who landed at the mouth of the Kennebec river. They erected buildings and constructed a vessel of thirty tons during that year they named "Virginia." They were favorably situated to construct the vessel, for one of the colonists was a ship carpenter. This body of colonists soon became discouraged; became involved in difficulties with the Indians, so that some went back the next year to England: others took the "Virginia" and sailed to the English colony at Jamestown, Va. The next vessel built in New England was the bark "Blessing of the Bay" of 60 tons burden on Mystic river, Mass., in 1631 for Governor Winthrop of the colony. The next year a vessel of 100 tons, a year later one of near 200 tons burden were built on the same river. Shipyards were soon located along the

Massachusetts coast where the fishing industry was carried on, for it was the commerce in the salted fishery product that much of the freight was obtained for the vessels trading to Europe, and the West Indies. This business in the fisheries was the main cause of the development of shipbuilding on the eastern coast at the early period, with the low cost of the finished vessel. This low price, placed upon their vessels by the colonial builders, was one of the reasons so many vessels were built for several years for foreign owners.

## NEW AMSTERDAM.

It is well known that the vessel in which Henry Hudson discovered the river which bears his name was called the "Half Moon." She was of small dimensions, being 74 1-2 feet length over all, beam 16.9 feet, and 10 feet depth of hold, with a draft of water of 7 feet. This vessel entered the lower bay on September 4, 1609: on the 11th he came into the upper bay, where he remained but one day, when he left for the upper part of the river, and arrived at the site of the present city of Albany on September 19, 1609. After a short stay he returned to the mouth of the river, and on October 4th following set sail for England. The first trading ships between Manhattan, or New Amsterdam, and Holland were the "Little Fox" and the "Little Crane," which were brought here in 1611 upon a speculating trading voyage, and spent a considerable time in bartering the trinkets and other trifles, so much coveted by the Indians for beaver and peltry, of which the country afforded a bountiful supply at the time. The adventure was a great success for the promoters, and we find the "Little Fox" making several voyages to the river at later dates.

Captain Adrian Block was sent out in 1613 in command of the ship "Tiger" by some merchants of Holland, in company with two other vessels to New Amsterdam, to trade with the Indians, but through an accident his ship takes fire while lying in the bay and preparing to return home. Nothing daunted by his misfortune he set to building a small yacht, so called, from the timber that was growing in such abundance on the island; and in all probability the construction of the vessel was carried on at the lower end of the island. The tools they had to work with were crude for the purpose, but the best they had at hand, and no doubt as good as was in general use at that day. It is not probable that there was anything better for shaping the timber than would be carried on board a vessel for doing repair work, in shape of tools. This vessel was the first one built at New Amsterdam, was 44 1-2 feet long, 16 1-2 feet wide and 16 tons burden and named "Onrest." She was used in exploring the coast for a distance to the north of Long Island Sound, and it was in this vessel that Capt. Block was the first, it is thought, of any Europeans, to have visited Block Island, that lies at the entrance of Long Island Sound. But little was done in shipbuilding for some time to which to call attention, until in 1631. The West India Company, who had the territorial right of trade with the colony, had built at Manhattan the ship "New Netherlands" "of about 600 tons," and it was in all probability the largest merchant vessel in the world at the time, and was sent to Holland. She was fitted for carrying thirty guns. We find that the record shows that the building of this vessel was severely criticised at a later date as bad management on the part of the West India Company. At a much later date the first shipyard is shown to be on the shore about two blocks inland from the present foot of Broad street, and known as Hunts shipyard.

One of the most notable maritime events in connection with the early history of Manhattan was the loss of the ship "Princess" and about sixty of her passengers and crew, some of the former being those whose names have been handed down to us in connection with affairs of the Dutch Province. This vessel left Manhattan for

Holland on August 16, 1647, having among her passengers William Kieft, who had been Director General of the Province, and Dominie Everardus Bogardus, the first clergyman established in the town. The latter married the widow Annetje Jans, who came into possession of the sixty-two acres of ground granted to her first husband in 1636, that in 1705 was leased to Trinity Church by the Colonial authorities, and that periodically is brought into public notice in the present day. Both Dominie Bogardus and ex-Director General Kieft, with some few other officers of the Province were lost with the vessel. The first shipwreck on the coast in the vicinity of Manhattan, of which we have any account, was in December, 1658, when the "Prince Maurice" went ashore about midnight on the south shore of Long Island at a place called Sicktewacky, near Fire Island inlet. The passengers were saved, but the ship was lost.

At the date of the capitulation of the Dutch proprietors in the city to the English in 1664 a number of property holders of the shipbuilding profession resided in a part of the town then known as "De Smits Valey," and afterward as the "Fly," along the shore road between Wall street and the present Franklin Square, or the line of Pearl street. The most of these shipwrights lived outside the water gate or city palisade at Wall street, while only one resided inside the enclosure. Whether they were all proprietors of shipyards there is no means of telling at this late date.

We find in a search through the old historical records of the Dutch occupation, references to many ships, but no data to show whether they were of domestic or foreign construction. There is one paper that details the work done at Manhattan during Governor Wouter Van Twiller's administration, that in 1633 consisted of the ship "Southerck" repaired and provided with new knees. Other carpenters have long worked on ships "Hope" of Greningen, and "Omlanden." The yacht

"Hope," captured in 1632, was entirely rebuilt, and planked up higher. The yacht "Prins William" has been built. The yacht "Amsterdam" almost finished. A large open boat. In the yacht "Wesel" an orloop and caboose were made. In the yacht "Vreede" the same. The boat "Omwal" at Fort Orange. The yacht with a mizzen sold to Barent Dircksen. The wood cutters' boat, divers' farm boats, and skiffs were sold to various parties. Also many boats and yawls made for the sloops. Moreover the carpenters constantly repaired and caulked the old craft."

We now come to the period of the English occupation of New Amsterdam, when its name was changed to New York. The population of the place did not exceed fifteen hundred inhabitants, and the number of dwellings on the island did not much exceed two hundred. There appears for some years no trace of activity in the shipyards, probably on account of the political conditions affected by the change of the administration, and also that during the Dutch occupation the island was for the most time used merely as a trading post, while under the English administration there was a more free and extended commercial spirit manifested. This change took some time to become general, and the city had in the meantime extended far beyond the palisade at Wall street, and largely increased in population. There was no longer a close corporation in control of the commerce of the city. There was no doubt many sloops built at this period for the trade on Hudson river, for there was considerable business done as far up the river as Albany.

The only shipbuilder there is any record of at this early date was John Latham, who purchased some "water lots" in 1701 in the vicinity of Dover street, and established a shipyard. He was no doubt the pioneer in that locality, that was so long known as the "Shipyards" district. In 1740 there were three shipyards in this locality, Daniel and John Latham, John Dallys, and

John Rivers. Lathams old dwelling house that stood at the corner of Cherry and Roosevelt streets was still standing in 1860. He seems to have had a disposition to invest in real estate at times in the city. The last record is of three large plots in 1752 on the shore front, near Roosevelt street, just west of where the stream running from Collect pond emptied into the East River. Shall refer to Latham again on the subject of timber.

Shipbuilding at New York could not have been a very inviting business to engage in at this early period, for the builders in the Massachusetts province could construct vessels at so much less cost, and that is one reason why they obtained so many contracts for vessels from foreign owners. The labor market was not in harmony with the local builders, though they no doubt built a few vessels for the inland waters. The General Assembly of the colony in 1718 presented to the Governor of the Province of New York and New Jersey, that it was of advantage to change the law so that vessels built in the province of British owners should be free from certain taxes on shipping, as it was at this time seen that the shipbuilding business was in a very depressed condition in the province for the amount of trade transacted, but it was not until 1736 when "shipbuilding, which in some of the neighboring provinces is carried on to a large extent, and has become a considerable part of their returns to Great Britain for many years, been much neglected and little used in this province." It was not only the new vessels for London merchants, but New England also sent across the Atlantic large shipments of shipbuilding timber. The Governor of the Province a few years later in an address to the legislative body of the province, said * * * "I have reflected on the decay of shipbuilding which for many years has been much regretted, but little attempted to be retrieved. I am not ignorant that many causes may be assigned for its decay, some of which, and particularly one, it is not in the power of the merchant or the builder at present to remove; nor do I see any other way whereby a remedy may be applied than by your aid. If the demands of the builder be higher than in the neighboring provinces the merchant will not, cannot built here without injuring himself. If the builder undertake the work at the same rate that is given in the neighboring provinces, he complains, and I fear with too much truth, he only labors to be undone for the excessive wages of carpenters which he must be obliged to hire, for want of apprentices, runs away with his profit, and he cannot take apprentices, being unable in his present poverty to maintain them. It is you alone who can supply a remedy to this evil, and you may do it at a very small annual expense, for I am persuaded that £200 a year given to shipbuilding, with apprentices at the rate of £8 a year, with each apprentice for six or seven years, will soon revive that necessary and useful work. It will make shipbuilders willing to take apprentices, enable them in their present necessities to maintain them, and to build for the merchant at as low a rate as in the neighboring provinces. You will then keep among you many thousand pounds which are now yearly exported out of the province by your neighbors, who are at present your carriers." * * * This plan of subsidy for the protection of the New York shipbuilder from the cheaper built vessels of his neighbors, does not appear to have been sufficiently inviting to the law-making power to place it upon the statute books. These existing conditions were largely overcome at a later date by the local shipping merchant and vessel owner becoming interested in some of the shipyards, where their new vessels were constructed and repairs made to those in service. Whether the apprentices were more largely employed in the shipyards than at an earlier date there is no record.

### TIMBER.

The early colonists and traders soon appréciated the wealth that lay in the fine timber that stood on the

Atlantic coast, for it was not only at New Amsterdam but at New England as well. The earliest shipment found from New Amsterdam was received at Amsterdam from Manhattan in November, 1626, on board ship "Arms of Amsterdam," considerable oak timber and hickory.

The first extended reference to the shipbuilding timber of New Netherlands is found in a Holland document of 1649, referring to the soil of the province: "It produces several kinds of timber suitable for the construction of houses *and ships*, be they large or small, consisting of various sorts of oak, to wit: Post oak, smooth white bark, gray bark, black bark, and still another sort, which by reason of its softness is called butter oak. * * * Various sorts of nut timber, hickory, large and small. This timber is very abundant here, and much used as firewood also, for which it is right well adapted. Chestnuts, three sort beeches, axe handle wood, ash, birch, pine, lathwood, alder, willow, thorn, with divers other species adapted to many purposes, but their names are unknown to us."

Colonists on arriving in the province in 1650 were after a certain formality granted and allowed certain privileges: "And they shall be at liberty, gratuitously, to cut and draw from the public forests as much firewood, and as much timber as they shall require for the construction of houses and vessels." This is an evidence that some shipbuilding was done at New Amsterdam at a very early date.

The shipment of shipbuilding timber does not appear to have been under the Dutch Administration a very profitable business. * * * "In regard to the timber that has been sent as freight, whoever has anything here to load ought not to be repulsed, but encouraged: if things are to succeed they must operate in that way. The timber was sent that labor may be supported. Though at present discredited and brought into disrepute, it will soon surmount the difficulty when improved. * * * That the ship should have arrived sooner home, ten or twelve days were employed in taking the timber in. It lay on the bank alongside the vessel and the crew undertook to haul and load it for 200 gl: it was the finest weather that could be expected. * * * Though the heavy freight absorb all the profit of the timber, yet it is better, that the people who are inclined to be industrious, should be accommodated."

Under the English occupation several shiploads of timber and plank were sent to the British Navy yards, "there being a great deal of timber in the country, chiefly oak, the white oak is the best; they build many ships with it." Sticks of timber for masts of vessels were sent at as late a date as 1700 to the parent country in large quantity. England had been so wasteful in the use of her timber for many years that they began to see they must look outside their local fields for a supply.

Earl Bellomont, Governor of the province, in a letter to the Commissioners of Trade and Plantations of England in 1699, gives us a view of the timber supply, and exportation going on, at the town at that time. "My thoughts have been so at work about naval stores and masts for the king's ships that understanding last spring from two honest Dutchmen that had found out a parcel of vast pines on one of the late grants of land by Col. Fletcher to Mr. Dellius, which they said were big enough for masts for the biggest ship in the world, I resolved to take an account of them, and for that end sent Mr. Schermerhorn, one of the Dutchmen that discovered them to me, and with him John Latham, an able shipwright, who learned his trade in one of the king's yards in England, to view them, and to take a survey of all the woods in that part of the province, I mean, to the northward of New York, up the Hudson river, the Mohacks river, and along the side of Corlears Lake, where Dellius, largest grant was. By my instructions Latham was to report what trees he found fit for masts, what pitch pines for making pitch, tar and rosin, and all other timber fit for building ships of war, as beams, planks, wale pieces and knees. Upon their return, which was just a month ago, they sent me the journal of their travel in the woods * * * and it is signed by Mr. Schermerhorn and Mr. Latham. I send the Lieut. Governor of New York's proclamation forbidding the cutting away of those great trees fit for masts for the king's ships. But in the province of New York people little mind proclamations or laws either. I am glad to find there are pines of eleven and twelve feet about, for either one of those sizes is big enough for a first rate ship, as I am informed, and I am satisfied the trees might be floated down the great fall, and then they will be the cheapest in the world, for they may be all floated down Hudson's river to the ship's side that take them in to carry them to England." This fall he mentions "is 600 yards broad, and at the highest part about 50 feet high * * * eight miles above Albany." It was not only from New York that timber for the British naval vessels was now being sent, but from New England as well in large quantities, where they were also building vessels for the merchant service for English owners. The next year Earl Bellomont shipped another cargo of timber by the ship "Fortune." "This vessel stands the king in £558 19s., New York money, * * * and Mr. Latham, the shipwright of best skill and experience here, values the ship at nearly £600 sterling. She is nearly nine years old * * * but the king will be no loser but a gainer, as I have ordered the matter, I mean, by sending home the ship laden with ship timber. The timber I have provided standing me in £467 7s. 4d. this money. * * * Also Capt. Deering for a character of the timber that is left behind on the wharf in this town, and they will tell Lordships 'tis better than that which is put on the 'Fortune,' for it seems Mr. Latham shipped that timber which first came to hand,

and did not choose the best." A little later he advises the Home office that he has made a contract for a supply of timber for masts for the king's naval vessels. "I have made a bargain with two men for masts * * * which if they will perform must prove the best bargain for the king that ever was yet made. * * * The articles, bonds and instructions are my own drawing, for I was forced at drawing them myself to keep this design secret from some ill people at Albany, who are wicked enough to hinder the good effects of such a bargain by persuading the Mohack Indians either not to part with their woods to the king, or to hold them up at an extravagant rate. * * * Some of the people at Albany upon my sending Mr. Latham and these two undertakers last year to view those woods began to practice with those Indians and persuade them that each of those great pines for masts was worth fifty beaver skins. Mr. Latham assures me that there are pines enough in those woods on the Mohack river to furnish the navy these thousand years to come. The twenty-four masts I have articled for will serve a first and second rate man of war. The biggest in Mr. Taylor's contract was 37 inches diameter. * * * I have agreed for two masts of 40 inches diameter, which will be a rarity when sent home. * * * I cannot but flatter myself that this bargain for masts is a very valuable service to the king and all his dominions: for here is a sufficient store for all. I believe I shall save the king £15,000 a year in the article of masts, boltsprits and yards: and more."

# CHAPTER II.

1784 TO 1820.

EARLY AMERICAN NEW YORK SHIPBUILDERS — THE "CLERMONT" AND HER BUILDER.

HEN the City of New York was freed from the presence and authority of a foreign military power on Nov. 25, 1783, under whose oppression it had suffered for about seven years, it was little else than a heap of ruins. During this period nearly all kinds of industrial occupations were wholly suspended, excepting those of military necessities. The wharves had been permitted to go to decay without any efforts being made to check their ruin, or to restore them when they became almost useless, excepting those used for military purposes. Both public and private buildings had been appropriated by the military authorities, and of course had been marred and defaced by such use. A large portion of the city was included in the burned district, which had been laid in ruins by two great fires that occurred during the early part of the war, and no attempts had been made since the fires to remove the ruins of the buildings. These long and painful years of its military occupation by the British troops had reduced the city to little more than a wreck of its condition at the beginning of the war. Previous to the commencement of hostilities the population of the city had reached over twenty thousand, but the occupation of the city by a foreign foe had reduced the number of permanent residents to less than half that number. Many of the dwellings of the refugees from the city were taken by the British war officers for military uses. For the purposes of a naval depot the shipyards at Dover and Roosevelt streets were occupied, and the adjacent ground was enclosed and houses erected for storage of material for repairs to the naval vessels. The shore front at this locality being well suited for the purpose, was used as a "careening yard" for vessels under repairs. Several of the dwellings situated on Cherry Hill, where Cherry street at present commences, were taken by the naval officers on shore duty for their private quarters, and for their offices. This locality at the outbreak of the Revolutionary War had some of the finest residences in the city. The mechanics for this service were brought from Great Britain. It will be borne in mind that there were many vessels engaged in bringing military supplies for the Army and the Navy during all these years, and these transports must receive greater or less repairs during every voyage: besides several naval vessels were kept at this port to convoy the transports from New York for a certain distance, and meet others coming to the westward, to prevent their capture by our privateers. This made it necessary to have a plant of some size at the base of operations, for the repair of all naval vessels and transports, as New York was at this period. There does not appear that there were any vessels built in the city for the merchant service during the seven years of British occupancy of the city. All the old shipyards seem to have passed out of existence, though the locality was still known as "the shipyards," for the owners had sought more congenial surroundings for their business, or had entered the service of the patriot army. So the city became during this period a vast military depot for the army and navy of the British Isles, and what commerce the city had was for their account, or its most loyal supporters. This is the only interval when the city did not have a ship yard from the Dutch occupation.

After the treaty of peace many of the families that had fled when the city fell into the hands of the enemy, returned, but not at once in sufficient numbers to make up the loss of the early exodus. But the revival of commerce, and the demand for the labor of mechanics of all kinds, with that of unskilled labor, attracted men from far removed points, several ship carpenters coming to the States from even as far as Canada to better their condition. In about five years after the restoration of peace the city began to show that it had gained in population all its losses of the war period, and that it would take its place as one of the foremost cities of the prospective Union of States. During this period there was a very limited amount of business done in this city in the construction of new vessels on account of the disturbed state of political affairs, foreign complications, and their effect upon the commercial interests of the new nation: it had just started out as an independent nation, and was trying to get its bearings.

That there were very limited facilities for shipbuilding at New York immediately after the close of the War of the Revolution is seen by the fact that the ship "Empress of China" built at Baltimore, Md., of 360 tons, and owned by Robert Morris of New York and Daniel Parker & Co., of Philadelphia, Pa., was cleared from New York City for China with a cargo of ginseng, being the first vessel from the States to open commercial intercourse with that eastern empire, on February 22, 1784. What was considered as a novelty in shipbuilding circles at the time was that this vessel had her bottom covered with sheet copper, being one of the earliest American vessels so fitted. The first American vessel from New York to Great Britain after the close of the war was the ship "Betsy" for London in May, 1784.

When our first frigates were designed there was no copper sheet mill in the United States that was able to supply the demand of the United States government for copper sheathing of these vessels, so the metal was obtained in Great Britain. The record in the Treasury department regarding the construction of these vessels says: "I furnished you with an estimate of the composition metal, sheathing copper, bolts and nails, bunting, and iron kitchens for the six frigates, all of which were ordered from Europe: and a note of the anchors, which last were postponed for a further inquiry, whether they could not be manufactured in the United States." The Navy department in 1801 advanced ten thousand dollars to Paul Revere and Son of Boston, Mass., "to erect works for manufacturing sheet copper," and under a contract had delivered in two years 350,000 pounds in bolts and sheets of copper for the vessels of the navy. This was the beginning of that industry on the scale of any importance to be noticed in this country, though Paul Revere had a foundry in 1792 where he "cast bells and brass cannon; manufactured sheets, bolts, spike and nails from malleable copper and cold rolled."[3] There were for some years later many vessels sent to Great Britain, that were built in the United States, to have their bottoms copper sheathed, as an export duty was placed on the metal by Great Britain, that with the freight made it less costly for vessels engaged in the foreign trade to be coppered in Great Britain. Sheathing copper was duty free.

Some of the surrounding conditions of shipbuilding during the latter part of the 18th century may be obtained where the Secretary of the Navy says in 1798 regarding the building of the naval vessels: "There can be no doubt entertained but the rise of the price of most, if not all, the materials and labor employed in building and equipping the frigates has added considerably to the expenditures. The rise of wages alone between the date of the first estimate and the time the frigates were launched, taking Philadelphia for example, was from 9 shillings to 15 shillings per day, and the rise in wrought iron, and hemp, about forty per cent." There was at this time, when the "President" was built, no navy yard at New York, only two wharfs at Cherry and Market streets, and buildings for storage of material for naval use, just above the private shipyards. This was but a temporary location for naval purposes until the property at Brooklyn was purchased for a navy yard in 1801. The Secretary also said: "Docks will be highly necessary in repairing our ships, to avoid the tedious, expensive, and sometimes dangerous operations of heaving down."

The shipbuilder of the colonial period, and for some years the American shipbuilder, had one great advantage in having the raw material for his structure so close to his hand. Was not the American wooden shipbuilder of the 19th century wasteful with his timber in his building operations, and for that reason the present generation is suffering for the want of such material for other purposes? The Secretary of the Navy in 1814 said: "When it is considered that one 74 gun ship requires 2,000 large oak trees, equal to the estimated produce of 57 acres, the importance of securing for public use all that valuable species of oak which is found only on the southern seaboard, is sufficiently obvious." Along the coast of Maine to North Carolina the white oak forests extended several miles inland, and the supply of hickory and white pine was abundant, and more so, for the local shipbuilders. Live oak was the product of the coast States below North Carolina, and it is doubtful if it was used for shipbuilding purposes much before 1750, for in that year a vessel built of live oak, and named "Live Oak," arrived at Charleston, S. C., and by the knowledge gained of the valuable properties of this timber for shipbuilding, a new era in that industry set in in that locality. The use of this kind of timber in the construction of vessels at New York was, in all probability, not until after the close of the War of the Revolution. The live oak for the first frigates built, was obtained at first by sending labor from the northern States to fell the trees, and cut them to partial shape on the ground, but this did not prove a success at first, as the workmen were unacclimated. This was the largest amount of live oak that had been sent to the shipyards of the northern States, for prior to this occasion but a small amount had been brought here. As early as 1799 there is record of vessels for sale that "were built of pasture oak, live oak, and locust; is composition bolted, copper fastened, and coppered to the bends."

With the increase of population the city began to spread out, and the farm land east of the shipyards was cut through by streets, lots laid out, and dwellings soon began to be built and occupied mostly by the industrial class of people. The old shipyards were crowded out by the expansion of the city, and the first move made toward Corlears Hook with this industry.

On account of the very incomplete record the earliest builder found has been Samuel Akerly, (or Ackerly), who built in 1792 at his yard, foot Market street, two vessels. At this time there were not more than thirty ship carpenters in the city. There was another builder named Thomas Cheeseman, father of Forman Cheeseman, who will be mentioned more fully at a later date, who had a yard at the same period, but little is known of his building operations. This Thomas Cheeseman may have been engaged in shipbuilding just prior to the Revolutionary War, for he was the owner of 75 feet shore front in 1772 between the present Pike and Rutgers streets, and it was this spot Forman Cheeseman occupied after he left the firm of Cheeseman and Brownne. There were two other shipbuilders, a few years later, Thomas Vail, and William Vincent, the former at one time having a yard foot Rutgers street. There were at this time six Lathams, all ship carpenters, and no doubt of the family of John Latham, who resided in the old ship yard vicinity, two of them builders, but what vessels there is no trace. The early vessels noted on another page were no doubt constructed by some of these named builders. At this time it was said, "The shipyards are all along Lombard (Monroe) streets. Beekmans, Tillous, Franklin and Ackleys wharfs betwixt the shipyards and Rutgers house." These builders were the pioneers of the New

York City shipbuilders just after the formation of the United States.

Samuel Ackerly was an owner of real estate in the vicinity of his shipyard, and as late as 1835 the city bought from his heirs a one-third interest in the water front at Pike street. The new shipyards began to locate further up the river in a few years, so that by 1800 we find Cheeseman and Browne, the latter the builder of Robert Fulton's "Clermont" in 1807, located at Cherry and Clinton streets, and a few years later Adam and Noah Brown, and Eckford and Beebe, in the same vicinity. Christian Bergh* was one of the early builders who opened a shipyard at Corlears Hook, for its found he purchased a lot of ground in 1799 of 23 ft. x 80 ft. on Crown Point street, that was on the river front, but too small for a shipyard, probably for a dwelling. He had a shipyard in that locality a few years later, but this may have been rented for his business, as other builders had done. He must have been very successful in business, for in 1810 we find he purchased in the immediate vicinity of his yard, "on the banks of the East River near a place called Corlears Hook" a plot of about 150 ft. x 200 ft. for thirteen thousand dollars, and about the same time six lots on Scammel street for $4,370. He was considered one of the solid men of the vicinity. The beach of this water front on Corlears Hook was the most used for bathing purposes of any on the east side of the city on account of its fine sandy bottom and the shelving shore, and was

*It has been mentioned by more than one writer that Christian Bergh, Jr., was appointed to superintend the construction of the frigate "President." This is an error, for the navy record shows a report where it says: "Statement of the progress made in building a frigate to carry 44 guns at New York under the direction of Mr. Foreman Cheeseman and Capt. Silas Talbot, Supt." The naval constructor did not make a contract to build the vessel, but was employed by the government, and they were taken "from the best qualified of their profession, and in order that the public should derive all the advantage of their whole time, they have been detached from all private pursuits by a liberal compensation, at the rate of $2,000 per annum." Christian Bergh's name does not appear in any of the naval papers of record for the building of the "President."

used by the members of the Baptist churches of the city in their religious immersion exercises, that drew large audiences to the spot on such occasions. These were the principal shipyards on the East River in 1805. At this time there were 117 shipwrights and ship carpenters in the city.* It was a year or so later, that one of those experiments in transportation of such a radical type of a full working size, was put under construction, and one that has had such a marked effect upon the transportation of passengers and goods over the whole civilized world. This was the construction of Robert Fulton's steamboat "Clermont."

### THE "CLERMONT" AND HER BUILDER.

Robert Fulton has justly received all the credit for *the combination*† of the several parts in making the first successful steamboat, the "Clermont," which comprised the application of the steam engine to the propelling agent in the shape of the vertical side wheels, while the builder of the hull of the vessel has been but little known or referred to as her constructor.

Charles Browne was born in London, England, August 24, 1766, and served some time in the British dock yards. This was at a time when Great Britain placed restrictions upon all of her subjects who were mechanics from emigrating to the United States, especially those who had received their instructions in "the art of shipbuilding" in the government dock yards, and this may account for his name having the affix of ne, as his parents' name was Brown. His name has been variously spelled. Cadwallader D. Colden in his "Life of Robert Fulton, 1817," in the list of steam vessels built under the direction of Robert Fulton, spells his name

*There were at the time of the allied trades, 14 small boat builders, 12 brass founders, 3 caulkers, 9 ship joiners, 59 riggers, 40 sail makers and 36 sawyers in the city.

†See Scientific American Supplement, Nov. 2, 1907, "Robert Fulton and the Side-Wheel Steamboat."

Brown. In all his conveyances of real estate his name is spelled with the affix: the record of all the registered vessels built by him show his name with the affix: the tombstone in St. Paul's Church yard covering the graves of his sister and his daughter shows the same spelling: and the death notices in the papers at the time of his decease have the name in the same form. This is sufficient evidence that Cadwallader D. Colden was not correct when he said Charles *Brown* built the "Clermont"; his name was Charles *Brownne* and as such he should be known. There is no record where he landed in this country, but it was during the spring of 1788: nor do we find for the early days in this country where he was employed, nor how far he was advanced in his trade. His name first appears in New York directory for 1794 as a shipwright. This was at the time the United States government was having built at New York the frigate "President," under charge of Naval Constructor Forman Cheeseman, who was subsequently his partner in the business of shipbuilding for some years, and it is more than probable he was employed in the construction of that vessel, that was discontinued when half finished. Work on this vessel was started again in 1799 and the whole completed in the spring of 1800 under the same naval constructor. During this year Forman Cheeseman and Charles Brownne opened a shipyard at what is now known as the block bounded by Montgomery, Clinton, Cherry, and Munroe streets about two blocks inland from where the N. Y., N. H. & H. Railroad Co. have their present freight docks. This appears to have been the first of the junior partner's business on his own account. This partnership continued until about 1805 or '06, when Brownne continued the business in his own name for several years. About 1804 the firm took another yard at the foot of Stanton street on what was known as Manhattan Island, that afterward became so famous as a shipbuilding center.

It is readily seen that the builder of the "Clermont's" hull had been associated in business with one of the foremost shipbuilders of New York at that time, and that his industrial experience had been very broad, for he not only had been engaged in naval work before coming to this country, but while in New York City was employed on the frigate "President," and also on merchant vessels. His employment in Great Britain and then in this country, under different principles of construction, must certainly have broadened his knowledge of the "art of shipbuilding." This may have been one of the reasons why Robert Fulton had engaged him to construct the "Clermont."

It seems at first sight of the subject as being remarkable that there has never been found any drawing of the vessel, nor the sketch of a proposed design, nor a cut of the vessel during her service, nor a contract for the construction of the vessel: but when surrounding conditions are examined it is found that the vessel was an experiment, and in all probability was constructed like many other experiments of a mechanical nature at a later date; it was started without any detail plans, but carried on step by step, worked out as it progressed in form, with possibly some alterations, until the finished structure was unlike what was first thought best for the purpose. The general design of the hull of the vessel, and the materials for its construction, were no doubt the suggestions of the builder. We nowhere find that Robert Fulton claimed to be a naval architect, though he had professed to be a civil engineer. He no doubt had a theoretical knowledge of naval architecture prior to building the "Clermont," that he had gained during his experiments of steam propulsion with his small experimental vessels, and also in his experiments with his submarine boat, and torpedos, but as a designer or a constructor he had no experience. Let there be borne in mind that Robert R. Livingston, who was the capitalist of the enterprise, had been engaged in experiments with the steamboat while Robert Fulton was in Europe, and no doubt his knowledge of the trials he had encountered in his efforts to obtain a proper propelling agent, was of much value to Robert Fulton in his making of the proper combination for the "Clermont."

Prior to the construction of the "Clermont" the longest merchant vessel built at New York was 120 feet in length, while the frigate "President" for the United States Navy was but 174 feet 10½ inches in length on the gun deck. The "Clermont" was 140 feet in length, being several feet longer than any former merchant vessel built at New York, and more than probable in this country. There was not alone the problem of design for a longer vessel, but for one to carry a fixed weight of engine and boiler, and of such a model* as to provide for the proper distribution of weights on a light draft of water.

The only account of any details of the building of the hull of this vessel, thus far brought to light, is furnished through The Marine and Naval Architect that was published in 1853 by John W. Griffiths, who was a New York shipbuilder, and whose father was a ship carpenter in New York City at the period the "Clermont" was building. This work says: "It may not be out of place to furnish a brief description of Mr. Fulton's first effort at steamboat building, more particularly when we are assurred that no mechanical drawing of the hull was ever made. The boat was 133 feet long, 18 feet wide and 7 feet deep, and was subsequently made 22 feet wide by adding a strip of four feet to her middle, which also increased her length to 141 feet. Her bottom was formed of yellow pine plank of 1½ inches thick, tongued and grooved and set together with white lead. This bottom was laid on a transverse platform and molded out with

*The so-called model of the "Clermont" in the Smithsonian Institute will no doubt be a curiosity to future generations, with its four sharp knuckles.

batten and nails to the form required. The shape being thus formed, floors of oak and spruce were placed across, the spruce floors being 4 in. x 8 in. and 2 feet apart, the oak floors being reserved for the engine space and the spruce for the ends, the oak floors being both sided and molded 8 inches. Her top timbers, which were of spruce and extended from a log which formed the bilge to the deck, were sided 6 inches and molded 8 inches at the heel, and both sided and molded 4 inches at the head. She had no guards when first built, and was steered by a wheel in a cockpit. * * * As no complete draft of the hull of this boat, either before or after she was widened, has ever been shown, the world cannot contrast all the improvements of nearly half a century."

A most valuable letter on the subject of the "Clermont" has been placed at the service of the writer by the owner of the letter, Mr. T. V. Hoffman, president New York Historical Society, from which extracts of the defects found in three months' service of the vessel are taken. This letter is an original from Robert Fulton to Robert R. Livingston, who was the associate of the former in this enterprise, and is dated at Washington, D. C., Nov. 20, 1807. The letter says in part: * * * "It is now necessary to consider how to put our first boat in a complete state for 8 or 10 years, and when I reflect that the present one is so weak that she must have additional knees and timbers, new side timbers, deck beams and deck, new windows and cabins altered, that she perhaps must be sheathed, her boiler taken out and a new one put in, her axles forged, and iron work strengthened; with all this work the saving of the present hull is of little consequence, particularly as many of her knees, bolts, timbers and planks could enter into the construction of a new boat. My present opinion therefore is that we should build a new hull, her knees and floor timbers to be of oak, her bottom planks of 2 inch oak, her side plank 2 inch oak for three feet high. * * *"

There is another paper bearing on the same subject from Judge Joseph Story, who was as a lawyer, one well read in maritime law at the time, and an Associate Judge United States Supreme Court during the early years of the "Clermont" service on the river. In a paper on "The Development of Science and Art" he says of Robert Fulton and the steamboat: "I have heard the illustrious inventor relate, in an animated and affecting manner, the history of his labors and discouragements. When (said he) I was building my first steamboat at New York the project was viewed by the public either with indifference or with contempt, as a visionary scheme. My friends indeed were civil, but they were shy. They listened with patience to my explanations, but with a settled cast of incredulity on their countenances. I felt the full force of the lamentation of the poet,

Truths would teach, or save a sinking land,
All fear, none aid you, and few understand.

As I had occasion to pass daily to and from the building yard while my boat was in progress, I have often loitered unknown near the idle group of strangers, gathering in little circles, and heard various inquiries as to the object of this new vehicle. The language was uniformly that of scorn, or sneer, or ridicule. The loud laugh often rose at my expense. * * * I invited many friends to go on board to witness the first successful trip. Many of them did me the favor to attend as a matter of personal respect, but it was manifest they did it with reluctance, fearing to be the partners of my mortification, and not of my triumph. I was well aware, that in my case there were many reasons to doubt of my success." * * *

Fulton refers to the hulls of the early steamboats built for him in his patent of February 11, 1809. To this time he had built the "Clermont" or "North River," had designed the "Car of Neptune," and had carried on some experiments of the resistance of bodies moving in water, being indebted for many of his tables in his patent to

Charnock's "History of Marine Architecture." His experience of more than a year in the practical operation of this vessel on her route, must have been of great value to him. He said in the patent, of the hulls: "To give room for the machinery, passengers and merchandise, I build my boats five or more times as long as their extreme breadth at the water line. The extreme breadth may be one-third from her bow, or in the middle, in which case the water line will form two equal segments of a circle united at the ends. To diminish the plus and minus pressure I make the bow and stern sharp to angles of at least 60 deg., and that the boat may draw as little water as possible I build it flat or nearly so on the bottom. * * * To prevent the boat making leeway she has leeboard or boards which are let down into the water while she is sailing: hitherto there have been two leeboards on each side of the boat, one on each side near the bow and one on each side near the stern."

There is one other authority from whom we may gain a little knowledge of the form of the hulls of the pioneer steamboats in this country, and that is from the "Treatise on the Steam Engine" by Prof. James Renwick* 1830, of Columbia College, where he says in referring to the success of the "Clermont" and John Stevens' "Phenix": "From that time to the death of Fulton, the steamboats of the Atlantic coast were gradually improved until their speed amounted to 8 or 9 miles per hour, a velocity that Fulton conceived to be the greatest that could be given to a steamboat. To this inference he was probably led by the observation of the increased resistance growing out of the wave raised in their front. His three earlier boats, "The Clermont," the "Car of Neptune," and the "Paragon" were flat bottomed, their bows forming acute

*Prof. Renwick, at the time of the North River of Clermont being in service, was an instructor in Natural Philosophy in Columbia College in New York City, and in 1814 was an officer in the Engineering Corps, U. S. Army.

curved wedges, the several horizontal sections of which were similar. His last boats had keels, but they were introduced for no other purpose than to increase their strength. In the boats constructed by his successors, after his death, a nearer approach was made to the usual form of a ship, but the waves still formed an important obstacle."

Putting all these facts and opinions together of the shape and construction of the "Clermont," it is manifest that it was an experiment of a radical form, and one that required much mechanical ability and experience to give the vessel its proper shape, so that the fixed weights could be properly placed for the vessel to float on an even keel, otherwise the vessel would have been far from a success. Some credit for this certainly should be given to the builder of the hull. If the trial had been a failure must not the designer and builder of the hull have shared the loss of credit for professional ability as a ship-builder? Designers or constructors of the hull of a successful steam vessel at the present day receive their share of credit for the vessel, and why should not Charles Browne receive honorable mention at least for his share of the skill in the construction of the "Clermont"?

The next steamboat Robert Fulton had built after the "Clermont" was the "Raritan," for J. R. and R. J. Livingston, by the builder of the "Clermont," to run from New York to New Brunswick, N. J. Fulton left a few details and a drawing of the vessel, in the former of which he says, "As you will have more and greater waves than the North River boat the wheel guards must be so constructed that the head of the wave shall not strike under them. I would finish them as here delineated: they are 4 feet from the water. Keelsons for the boiler 8 feet 6 inches from outside to outside; keelsons for the machinery 7 feet from outside to outside: hatchway to let in the boiler 8 feet 4 inches wide by 21 feet long." In the drawing for this vessel there is the hollow trough or keel noted in the contract for the "Car of Neptune." There is not the sharp angular meeting of the bow and the stern lines with the side lines of the vessel, as called for by a so-called model; nor do the leeboards show on the drawing.

While Fulton was having the "Raritan" built he entered into a contract with Charles Brownne in October, 1808, on his own account, for the construction of the second steamboat for the Hudson river line, that was named "Car of Neptune": this was only a few months after the "North River" x "Clermont" was enlarged. This contract appears to be the first paper of authority giving any of the details for the construction of Robert Fulton's early steamboats. The following copy was made from the original contract, that was placed in the hands of the writer, and it shows many of the provisions for her construction. The plan of the vessel referred to cannot be found.

"New York, October the first, eighteen hundred and eight. * * * I, Charles Brownne, shipbuilder of the City of New York, do engage to build and deliver to Robert Fulton, Esq., or his order, a boat of the following dimensions: One hundred and fifty-seven feet long on her bottom, one hundred and sixty-three feet long on her deck, extreme breadth of her bottom eighteen feet, extreme breadth on her deck twenty-two feet, formed exactly agreeable to a plan of Robert Fulton's, dated 4th September last, and now in my possession.

"Details nearly as follows:

"Bottom perfectly flat and hogged up in a regular curve of 3 inches from stem to stern. A hollow trough or keel amidships 100 feet in length, to draw off the water, as in the present boat. Every third or fourth timber of oak, all lower knees of oak. All oak to be of the best seasoned white oak, and all parts where particular strain lies, to be of best seasoned white oak. To plank her bottom, and three feet up each of her sides from the bottom with the best seasoned 3 inch pine, rabbetted together: the remainder of her sides and deck to be of 2-inch pine, long lengths and well seasoned.

"To have all the joiners' work done in the best New York style, and of seasoned stuff. To have the plumbing, painting and glazing finished equal if not superior to the present boat. To finish her interior parts, that is, cabins, berths, lockers, drawers, bars, pantries and all things agreeable to the before mentioned drawing. To finish the wheel guards complete, and a cover to each wheel. To fix the oak frame to receive the machinery; to finish its iron work, and all the iron work of the boat, *but to have nothing to do with the machinery or mason's work.* To furnish and thoroughly secure the diagonal braces. To finish and fit four leeboards complete, but not their blocks and rigging. To furnish two masts with their booms, studding sail booms and yards, but not rigging, sails, anchors or cables. To furnish a capstan, rudder, tiller and tiller wheel. To furnish davits to suspend the boats. Hatches with coverings of oil cloth or tarpaulin to cover the machinery and skylights: and in fact to execute everything detailed in Mr. Fulton's letter dated 9th of August last. To launch her and deliver her safe and sound in all her parts in April next for the sum of eight thousand two hundred dollars.

Payable as follows:

$1,000 8th of Oct.
1,000 8th of Nov.
1,000 1st of Jan'y.
1,000 1st of March
1,000 when launched.

After the launch

3,200 in three bills.

$1,000 in 2 mos. $1,000 in 4 mos. $1,200 in 6 mos.

"And if while the hull of the boat is building Mr. Fulton should make any alterations in the arrangements of his cabins, or interior work, I agree to execute them agreeable to his future directions, provided such alterations should not necessitate me to undoe any part of the work which may at the time be fixed, nor add evidently to the quantity or expense of the work here contracted to be executed.

"I agree to these conditions,

"ROBERT FULTON."

Witness

LEWIS CLAPHAM.

This vessel was completed and placed in service on the New York and Albany line in September, 1809.

It appears the further the search is made into conditions surrounding the two owners of this vessel, that the more confusing it becomes to obtain a clue to why there has never been found a cut, painting or drawing of the "Clermont" while afloat. Here we find those having all interest in the enterprise to be men of learning, large business experience, and wide knowledge of the world by travel, for that period. They were also members of the Academy of Arts, and of the American Philosophical Society, Robert R. Livingston being president of the former society many years. Robert Fulton was originally a portrait painter, and his skill at drawing and in water colors was well known at the time. Now, why with all this talent for painting and drawing, and his experience had been in the mechanical line in the latter, did Fulton neglect to leave a likeness in some form of the "Clermont" while in service? There are no individual cuts of steam vessels of any value until 1814 found in any publication, though some of the advertisements of the steam boat companies as early as 1810 contained a cut that served for any steam vessel. The first copper plate engraving having a steam vessel is in the "Portfolio" of November, 1813. This was intended in all probability for the "Paragon." Steel plate engravings came in later. As for wood cuts they were made at this time by only one man in this country, Dr. Alexander Anderson of New

York, who was at the time a member of the Academy of Arts with Livingston and Fulton. The earliest individual cut of any of Fulton's steamboäts is that of the "Paragon," engraved by Dr. Anderson and found in Vol. 2 of the American Medical and Philosophical Register of 1814, with descriptive matter by R. R. Livingston. Why we have no likeness of the "Clermont" while in service, will always remain a mystery past finding out.

The first cuts of the "Clermont" that have thus far been found, having any authority attached to them are

STEAMBOAT "CLERMONT."

the two on pages 34 and 35. The first one is from the Mechanics Magazine of New York of August, 1833, a high class mechanical journal of its day, which says in part: * * * "We now insert a copy from a drawing made by himself (Robert Fulton) and which may be considered as descriptive of the first successful application of steam in navigation. Since the above was in type, Capt. Davis Hunt, who was the commander of the boat, has seen the engraving and pronounces it correct in every particular." This Capt. Hunt was at the time of the "Clermont's" first being placed in service a mariner living in New York City, and is the captain of the vessel of which there has been some doubt. The other cut, without any sails spread on the vessel is from a Tourists Guide of 1844 given to the writer many years ago by late Capt. T. D. Wilcox of Ithaca, N. Y., who was a cabin boy on the "Paragon," one of the Fulton or Monopoly boats as early as April 1818, who claimed the cut was "the best picture of the vessel I have seen." The pennant shown on the foremast was made in the original with lead pencil by

THE "CLERMONT."

the captain in the writer's presence, and is the only change he made in the cut. Capt. Wilcox was in service on Long Island Sound prior to 1840, and later had a line of passenger steamboats on Cayuga Lake for several years.

It is readily seen that there is a great similarity in the form of the vessels presented in the two cuts. There is the same general form of joiner work on the main deck, though the vessel with sails has more shear to her deck, with about the same freeboard. One feature that is recognized in both cuts is the balance wheel of the engine being placed outboard but inside the water wheel. With such a marked similarity, and from sources not related in any particular whatever, separated by several years, and endorsed by those who were personally familiar during the early stage with the subject, it can with confidence be said the "Clermont" was in outward appearance very similar to these cuts.

Henry Eckford, who was a Scotchman, had served three or four years at his trade under his uncle, who was a shipbuilder at Quebec, Canada. He came to the United States in 1796, and after a few years' employment in this city built one vessel in Brooklyn in 1801, and by 1803 was in partnership with Edward Beebe under the firm name of Eckford and Beebe, and began building vessels at their yard near the foot of Jefferson street, where they built four or five vessels, two of them being ships for John Astor of New York. Henry Eckford, through his thorough knowledge of his trade, and skill in designing a vessel, built up a reputation in a few years as a first-class shipbuilder. He had not been taught the higher branches of the trade, but taking advantage of his practical experience he made many changes in the forms of his vessels that proved of value. His partnership with Edward Beebe ended in 1809. When the war of 1812-14 came on he had a well-equipped yard, but the building of merchant vessels coming to a close for a time, the Navy department obtained his services, and he was sent to the northern lakes to take full charge of the construction of the naval vessels on these bodies of water, where he remained during the period of hostilities. He came back to New York, opened his yard again, and built several vessels for the merchant service up to about 1825, among them being the first steam vessel built especially for ocean service, the "Robert Fulton" in 1819 for Dunham & Co., for the trade between New York and the island of Cuba. He was also employed in 1819-20 by the Navy department as Naval Constructor in charge at the Brooklyn Navy Yard, but official life was not in harmony with his advanced business ideas, and he handed in his resignation after the completion of the frigate "Ohio" of 2,740 tons. He was no doubt the ruling spirit in the shipbuilding line in New York City at this time, and had large influence in naval construction, so much so that in 1825-26 he built in connection with other builders, foot Stanton street, four 44 gun frigates for navies of South American governments. He was largely interested in many commercial corporations in the city, some proving very profitable investments, but one being the cause of the loss of most of his wealth that was subsequently recovered through wise investments. He continued in the business world until the Turkish government made him an offer to assume charge of their navy yard for the construction of their naval vessels, which he accepted, and left New York for Constantinople in June 1831, but only one vessel was built there under his supervision, as he died there in November, 1832.

It must not be thought that all science entered into the calculations for the design of a new vessel at this period, for the art of shipbuilding still lingered with them. The old method of "cut and try" from the building of some former vessel for a similar service was most generally made use of. This was during the chalk period. Instruments for the drawing of a vessel on a small scale were expensive, and conditions were not favorable for their general use in a ship yard, though we find by an advertisement in a New York paper of 1745, Anthony Lamb, mathematical instrument maker of this city, had for sale, besides quadrants, compasses, gauging rods; "drawing pens, shipwrights draught bows, bevels, squares and other small work." Most of these were no doubt imported instruments. It was only after several years of advancing step by step that scientific instruments began to come into use in this country in the designing of vessels to any extent, and the construction of our vessels was placed on a higher plane.

Forman Cheeseman commenced building vessels in his yard that was located near the foot of the present Rutgers street prior to 1800, and at a later date was associated with Charles Brownne where they built several fine vessels for that day, a few being the ships "Silenus" of 400 tons, the "Triton" of 340 tons, and the "Illinois" of 396 tons. Soon after this the former retired from the business of the firm, and the remaining partner continued the business in his own name. Cheeseman now had a yard for some years near foot Rutgers street. The establishment of new shipbuilding plants was further uptown about this time, but Crown Point, or Corlears Hook, as more generally known, was occupied with shipbuilding yards for several years. It was in this vicinity where the first of the large marine engine works, the Allaire Works, was located in the early days of steam navigation, and continued in active operation for more than forty years on the original site. This Forman Cheeseman was one of the very few naval architects and shipbuilders in the city, at the opening of the nineteenth century, who had a reputation of a high order for designing and construction, beyond their own locality. Philadelphia was considered at this time to be the one city in the United States having the best talent for designing and constructing sea going vessels, as it was the center of the most progress in the arts and sciences in the country, but in a few years New York City made such rapid strides in the industrial line that the shipbuilding industry of Philadelphia was no longer in the lead.

When Charles Brownne opened his yard on Manhattan island this locality was on the outskirts of the city, but very few dwellings being then beyond Corlears Hook on the east side of the city. This property was part of the James Delancey estate, that was forfeited to the people of New York State by his loyalty to the British cause during the War of the Revolution, and sold by the Commissioners of Forfeitures. Charles Brownne was one of the few shipbuilders of that date in the city, and was thought to be one of the most progressive in that trade in New York at the time. This Manhattan island has a local as well as a national historical interest, from the fact that it was on these grounds where Robert Fulton's "Clermont," the first successful steamboat in the world, was built in 1807, and where the first steam war vessel in any navy, the "Fulton the First," or "Demologos," was constructed in 1814 for the United States Navy by Adam and Noah Brown. All of Robert Fulton's steamboats were built by Charles Browune up to the time of Fulton's death, and after that for a time the steamboats of the North River Steamboat Company were built by Adam and Noah Brown and Henry Eckford. Charles Brownne in 1810 moved his yard to a lot 92 feet in width on northeast corner Water and Montgomery streets, the property of Henry Rutgers, the shore front in this locality at the time not being filled out completely beyond Water street. He remained here until about 1822, when he became timber inspector. Fortune did not favor him in his later days. He died in September, 1831. The property he had occupied on Manhattan island had been purchased in November, 1807, by Adam and Noah Brown, who occupied most of it after his removal. Henry Eckford also occupied a small portion of it. This Manhattan island was an oasis of solid ground, several acres in area, close by the river shore. On three sides of it were salt meadows or marshes, and on its eastern border flowed the waters of the East river. Being almost completely isolated from the shore of the island of Manhattan, it had been called an island, and for the sake of distinction had been known from early times as Manhattan island. With the progress of the city the salt marshes were filled in, the shore line was advanced into the river, and Manhattan island disappeared from the map of the city. The accompanying map will give a fair idea of the location of this historic spot at an early day.

Adam and Noah Brown commenced business in 1804 by taking a sub-contract from Thomas Vail, having a yard at the time foot of Montgomery street, to construct a ship for the European trade. They built several vessels during the next ten years, in the meantime locating

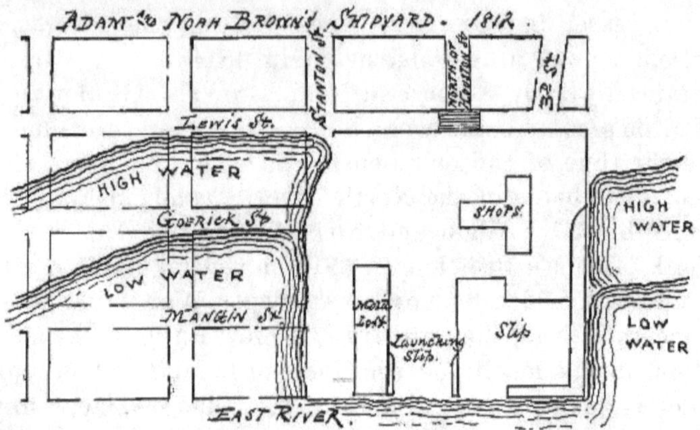


on Manhattan Island, for the latter part of this time was a comparatively lively period in shipbuilding in New York, some of the vessels being as large as 450 tons each. During this time there were other builders who were very actively engaged in the construction of vessels for our merchant marine, but none were more so, or had so extensive a plant as A. & N. Brown.

The War of 1812 with Great Britain now came on, and the shipyards of the city were almost destitute of new orders, the unfinished work at the outbreak of hostilities being soon completed. This threw the mechanics for a time on their own resources, but as the naval operations on the northern lakes soon began to assume an active form many of the ship carpenters were sent to the lakes to construct the naval vessels for our navy on those bodies of water, the work being under the general supervision of Henry Eckford, with Noah Brown in charge on

Lake Erie. In 1814, near the close of the war, there were 800 ship carpenters and other employees of the shipyards at work on the Northern lakes on these naval vessels, a large number being from New York and vicinity.

Robert Fulton in 1811 sent a ship carpenter of ability at his trade, from New York to take charge of building the hull of the first steamboat on the Western rivers at Pittsburg, Pa., the mechanics for performing the work being those in the West who were accustomed to building the barges and flat boats for those waters. After the close of the war, and before there was a great demand for labor in the coast shipyards, there was a call from the West for experienced ship carpenters, and fifty of that trade were sent from New York to the Ohio river, some locating at Cincinnati, Ohio, and others at Jeffersonville, Indiana. These men were the pioneers of the skilled labor in the shipyards on the Western rivers. They carried with them their Eastern practice of large and heavy timber for the structure of a vessel, but experience soon convinced them that this type of vessel for the shallow waters of the Western rivers was unsuitable, but they soon adapted themselves to the changed conditions, and constructed vessels more fitted for the service they were to perform. There were also ship joiners, as well as machinists, such as they were at that day, that emigrated to the Western States from New York City at this early period, that became prosperous at their trade in their new situation. They went there at the first call for skilled labor from the eastern shipyards, and their business grew up with the rapid increase of population in the Western States.

Soon after the close of the war in 1814 there came a demand in the coast cities for larger vessels to engage in the foreign trade, so that by 1816 there was built at New York the first of the packet ships that were especially designed for passengers and freight, for the Black

Ball Line in the New York and Liverpool trade. As the dimensions of these early packet ships have never been given, the figures for a few of the earlier vessels have been taken from the records of the New York Custom House; they were not so long as our three masted schooners of to day.

"Amity" 1816. Forman Cheeseman, builder. 382 tons. $106^1$x$28^6$x$14^3$. Owners, Isaac Wright, William Wright, Benjamin Marshall and Jeremiah Thompson.

"James Munroe" 1817. Adam Brown builder, for his own account. 424 tons. $118^1$x$28^8$x$14^1$. Purchased in 1818 by Wright & Co., of Black Ball Line. Had two decks and three masts.

"Manhattan" 1819. Sidney Wright, builder. 390 tons. $110^1$x$28^3$x$14^1$. Owner, Samuel Hicks.

"China" 1819. Adam and Noah Brown, builders. 533 tons. $122^1$x$31^4$x$15^8$. Two decks and three masts. Owner, Samuel Hicks.

"Albion" 1819. Sidney Wright, builder. 434 tons. $113^6$x$29^4$x$14^8$. Owners, Black Ball Line. Isaac Wright & Co.

"James Cropper" 1819. Sidney Wright, builder. 495 tons. $120^1$x$30^5$x$15^3$. Owners, Isaac Wright & Co.

Tench Coxe, who was the assistant of Alexander Hamilton, Secretary of the Treasury under George Washington, and a most able advocate of American manufactures, wrote at this period of American shipbuilding: "Shipbuilding is an art for which the United States is peculiarly qualified by their skill in construction and by the materials with which this country abounds: and they are strongly tempted to pursue it by their commercial spirit, by the capital fisheries in their bays and on their coasts, and by the production of a great and rapidly increasing agriculture. They build their oak vessels on lower terms than the cheapest European vessels of fir, pine and larch. The cost of an oak vessel in New England is about 24 Mexican dollars per ton fitted for sea: a fir-built vessel in the ports of the Baltic costs 35 Mexican dollars: and the American ship will be much the most durable. The cost of a vessel of the American live oak and cedar, which will last if salted in her timbers, thirty years, is only 36 to 38 dollars in our different ports: and an oak ship in the cheapest part of England, Holland or France fitted in the same manner will cost 55 to 60 dollars. In such a country, the fisheries and commerce with due care and attention on the part of the government must be profitable. * * * The best double deck or galley-built ship with live oak timbers, with white oak plank on their bottoms, and either that timber or yellow pine for their top sides, can be built and fitted for taking in cargo at 34 dollars per ton: and as good a vessel cannot be procured in Great Britain, France or Holland under 55 or 60 dollars. As the building of coasting and fishing vessels, boats in new forms for our improved inland navigation, vessels on various construction for public service, and for a very diversified foreign trade, will not only keep the art of shipbuilding at its present height, but will advance it in all respects. It appears to be very doubtful whether we should anxiously desire to supply foreigners with such cheap means of rivalling us in the carrying trade and fisheries. Our ship and boat yards are not confined to one spot, but are more diffused than formerly. There is no State in which the citizens do not pursue the business, and it is commenced upon the Western waters. Before the Revolution about one half our vessels were paid for by a barter of credit goods for the labor and skill of the artificers, instead of which he now generally receives weekly payments in solid coin."

With the demand for increased tonnage in 1816 came the call for more ship carpenters, but the supply was not equal to the demand of the times, for the shipbuilders of other coast cities had the same call for new vessels. This condition had been anticipated prior to the War of 1812-14 by a few New York builders in a small way, in taking a larger number of apprentices under instructions of "the art and mystery of shipbuilding," but it was not carried to an extent to be of much service to the builders until it was put in operation more generally after the war. Some of these apprentices became the best mechanics in the yards, and subsequently several of them operated ship yards of their own, in some cases being aided financially by friends interested in marine affairs, and employed at times several gangs of ship carpenters and other mechanics on the vessels under construction. These apprentices were mainly those who came into the business on the flood tide of the industry, and when it was nearing its height were in a position to take advantage of the industrial boom. By 1822 this scarcity of labor had been largely overcome through the apprenticeship system, and partly through the influx of foreign skilled labor from Europe and Canada. But a change came later on.

With the large demand for new vessels at this period more yards were opened. Christian Bergh, Jr., who had been on the northern lakes during the War of 1812-14 soon began active operations at his larger yard, and in 1825 the register of vessels built at that yard show that Christian Bergh, Robert Caruly and Jacob A. Westervelt were the master builders, which would imply the two latter having an interest in the business. They built but few steam vessels and these of small size. Christian Bergh retired from business in 1837, and was succeeded by his sons Henry and Edwin Bergh, who continued the business until just after their father's death in 1843, when the yard was closed for shipbuilding purposes. Isaac Webb, the father of William H. Webb, also began business on his own account near Corlears Hook about 1818. He had been instructed in his trade under Henry Eckford.

The apprenticeship system now began to bear fruit from the original introduction of the system by the builders at that period. It was a little later when steam vessels were constructed for other service than river navigation, as in the case of the "Savannah," built originally as a sailing vessel but altered to a steam vessel, and the "Robert Fulton," that ran from New York to Cuba, that by 1824, when the free navigation of the waters of the United States with steam vessels was decided by the United States Supreme Court, there were sufficient number of ship yards in the city, that were fully equipped for all the demands for the vessels required, and having better methods of construction than were adopted when the "Clermont" was built. New blood had come into the business and brought with them new ideas, or developed them after their term of instruction had expired, that were improvements on those methods of construction they had been taught during their term of apprenticeship. While these changes were not radical in the main, still they were a step forward. Like all other innovations, they were often looked upon at first by those of larger experience with grave doubts as to their merit, but their worth in many cases was soon recognized at their true value.

As showing the activity of the business in New York in 1824 may be quoted a report of an inspection made of the work then in hand during the latter part of the year. "In passing up the river a few days since I had the pleasure to count the number of vessels on the stocks at Corlears Hook and Manhattan Island, and ascertained it to be twenty, besides several fine ships which were launched last week. Among the vessels on the stocks are seven ships and four steamboats."

### REGISTERED SHIPS BUILT AT NEW YORK.

The following list is part of the registered vessels

built at this port by the most prominent builders of the periods, for 40 years subsequent to the close of the Revolutionary War. It is only laid before the reader to show the size of our vessels engaged in the foreign trade a century ago, with the builders' names.

"New York" built in 1788 of 243 tons. "Cheeseman" in 1791 of 274 tons. "Hare" in 1792 of 280 tons. "Ontario" in 1796 of 500 tons. "Canton" in 1799 of 518 tons. "Camilla" in 1799 of 397 tons. No record can be found who built these vessels.

Samuel Ackerly.

"Manhattan" in 1800 of 666 tons or $130^1$x$34^3$x$17^4$. "Fanny" in 1792 of 238 tons. "Samson" 1792 of 304 tons.

Eckford & Beebe.

"Magadalene" in 1805 of 355 tons. "Gold Hunter" in 1806 of 296 tons. "Beaver" 1805 of 427 tons. "Concordia" 1807 of 280 tons. "Mexican" 1808 of 294 tons. "Eliza Gracie" in 1809 of 420 tons.

Henry Eckford.

"Sam Elam" in 1800 of 324 tons. "Hennless" in 1809 of 554 tons. "Hannibal" in 1810 of 522 tons. "Hector" in 1818 of 380 tons. "Regulus" in 1818 of 877 tons. "Isabella" in 1820 of 468 tons. "Henry Astor" in 1820 of 377 tons. "Hercules" in 1822 of 497 tons. "Crawford" in 1824 of 289 tons. "Fabius" in 1822 of 432 tons. "Com. Chauncey" in 1822 of 387 tons. "Robert Fulton," steamship, 1819 of 702 tons.

Christian Bergh, Jr.

"Galloway" in 1807 of 344 tons. "Canton" in 1809 of 408 tons. "Gypsy" in 1809 of 207 tons. "Don Quixotte" in 1823 of 260 tons. "Ed Quesnel" in 1824 of 388 tons. "Paris" in 1824 of 338 tons. "El Bonaffee" in 1824 of 325 tons.

Adam & Noah Brown, and Noah Brown.

"Frances" in 1804 of 292 tons. "Swift" in 1805 of 289 tons. "Trident" in 1805 of 460 tons. "Boneta" in 1806 of 263 tons. "Maria Theresa" in 1807 of 330 tons.

"Pacific" in 1807 of 384 tons. "Tonquin" in 1807 of 269 tons. "Phorion" in 1807 of 265 tons. "Mentor" in 1808 of 257 tons. "America" in 1809 of 493 tons. "Chinese" in 1809 of 301 tons. "Highlander" in 1810 of 275, tons. "Aricola" in 1810 of 283 tons. "Colt" in 1810 of 228 tons. "Ontario" in 1812 of 527 tons. "James Munroe" in 1817 of 424 tons. "Horatio" in 1818 of 865 tons. "China" in 1818 of 533 tons. "Ajax" in 1821 of 370 tons. "Montano" in 1822 of 365 tons. "American" in 1822 of 339 tons. "Lewis" in 1823 of 412 tons. "Sabina" in 1823 of 412 tons. "Natchez," steam schooner, in 1823 of 206 tons. "Diamond" in 1823 of 491 tons. "William Byrnes" in 1824 of 517 tons. "Nassau" in 1824 of 407 tons. "Manchester" in 1825 of 561 tons.

Sidney Wright.

"Marcus" in 1818 of 283 tons. "Manhattan" in 1818 of 390 tons. "Albion" in 1819 of 434 tons. "James Cropper" in 1819 of 495 tons. "Rounlus" in 1820 of 232 tons. "William Thompson" in 1821 of 495 tons, or $120^1$x$30^3$x$15^6$. "Liverpool" in 1822 of 496 tons. "Columbia" in 1822 of 492 tons.

Fickett & Crockett, and Samuel Fickett.

"Savannah," pioneer steamship of 319 tons, or $98^6$x$25^{10}$x$14^2$. "Panther" in 1821 of 370 tons. "Maria" in 1821 of 418 tons. "Hannibal" in 1822 of 440 tons. "London" in 1822 of 407 tons. "Hudson," 1822, of 368 tons. "Leeds" in 1823 of 408 tons. "Herald," 1823, of 395 tons. "Shenandoah," 1823, of 475 tons. "York" in 1825 of 433 tons.

Brown & Bell.

"William Tell" in 1821 of 367 tons. "Orbit" 1821 of 384 tons. "New York" in 1822 of 516 tons. "Baltic," 1822, of 409 tons. "Henry" in 1823 of 287 tons. "Canada," 1823, of 545 tons. "Pacific" in 1824 of 586 tons. "Washington" in 1825 of 741 tons.

Blossom, Smith & Demon.

"Phocion" in 1822 of 522 tons. "Circassian," 1822, of

298 tons. "Harvard," 1822, of 336 tons. "Fanny" in 1823 of 390 tons. "Corinthian," 1823, of 401 tons. "Mary Lord," 1823, of 476 tons. "Balize," 1823, of 192 tons, steam schooner. "William Brown" in 1824 of 559 tons.

Thorne & Williams.

"Carolina" in 1822 of 80 tons, steamboat. "Europa" in 1823 of 369 tons. "Gen. Putnam" in 1824 of 418 tons.

Isaac Webb & Co.

"Superior" in 1822 of 575 tons. "Splendid" in 1823 of 642 tons. "Silas Richards," 1823, of 454 tons. "Oliver Ellsworth" in 1824, New York and Hartford steamboat, 227 tons.

Charles Brownne.

Besides the steamboats for Robert Fulton, ships "Star" in 1812 of 409 tons. "Cincinnatus" in 1818 of 373 tons. "London Packet" in 1819 of 320 tons.

It has been generally thought the "Superior" and the "Splendid," built by Isaac Webb & Co. in 1822 and 1823 respectively, were the largest ships built in this country at that period, but that is an error, for we find there were built in this city prior to either of these vessels, three ships either one much larger than the "Superior" or the "Splendid." They were the "Curiazo," built in 1817 by Forman Cheeseman for Paul Delano of New York of 851 tons, or $139^1x37^1x18^7$, having two decks and three masts; the "Horatio," built in 1818 by Adam & Noah Brown for own account, of 865 tons, or $138^1x37^9x18^{10}$, and sold for East India trade; and the "Regulus," built also in 1818, of 877 tons, or $147^1x36^6x18^8$, by Henry Eckford for own account, and sold to Peter Harmony and others, with an interest by the builder. This vessel was built wholly of live oak and pierced for 28 guns. These were the largest sailing vessels built here for several years.

That some of the New York shipbuilders were fortunate in accumulating a share of this world's goods we find from a survey of the assessment for personal taxes in this city. Adam and Noah Brown, each in 1815 for $15,000, Charles Brownne for $7,000 in 1815, and Henry Eckford for $30,000 in 1815, and $50,000 in 1820. These builders were at the same time interested in the development of real estate on the east side of the city that was now building up very rapidly. Noah Brown and Henry Eckford appear to have been impressed with the value of unimproved real estate in the "Out Ward," for there is the record of many purchases and sales by them at a very early period.

# CHAPTER III.

1820 to 1840.

PERIOD OF LARGE DEVELOPMENT IN SHIPBUILDING—MARINE RAILWAY AND DRY DOCKS—TOOLS.

Y 1820 the country had recovered in great part from the industrial depression of the late war, and the wise legislation that had been enacted for the protection of American industries had been a means of bringing capital to investment in the further development of steam navigation on our rivers. By 1824 the new shipyards that were opened had all been located above Corlears Hook, and in fact there were a few at and about Manhattan Island, for the city was now building up very rapidly on the East River side, taken up mainly by the mechanical classes. At this time the new firm of Brown & Bell, who were among the best for many years in constructing sailing and steam vessels, were located where Adam and Noah Brown had been, Smith & Demon were at Fourth street, Isaac Webb & Co. at Stanton street, and Lawrence & Sneeden, whose specialty was river steamboats, and who had a high reputation as builders, were at Corlears Hook.*

The number of vessels in 1824 in service had increased so largely, for the foreign as well as the coastwise and internal navigation and their size so much greater than a few years before, that some better means of preparing a vessel for inspection or repairs of the hull below the water line had to be made than the usual "heaving down" process then in use. There was at this

*The marsh surrounding Manhattan island extended along the shore to about 10th street, and inland in irregular lines to about Avenue B, with three large water courses running through it to the river. It was filled in during this period.

time no dry dock nor marine railway for taking out a vessel from the water for repairs in this country, either for the merchant service or the naval fleet. There was at the time only one resort, and that was with our naval vessels and large merchant vessels, in sending them to European dry docks when coppering of the bottom or serious repairs were made necessary. It was at this time that the first marine railway was put in operation in this country, but whether in New York City or Salem, Mass., is a question, more than probable by a few months in the former city. Robert Fulton is said to have had a railway for the purpose of repairing his vessel, but of its design there is no record. The New York Dry Dock Company was chartered by the New York Legislature in 1825 with banking privileges, and a capital of $700,000, to construct a dry dock at New York, but instead they built a marine railway for taking vessels out of the water for repairs. This company was brought into existence by the co-operation of the owners of the large sailing vessels, some of the owners of the Black Ball line of packets, to avoid the disadvantages to themselves of "heaving down" their vessels when requiring repairs. This marine railway was located at the foot of East 10th street, was 300 feet in total length, and was operated at first by horse power, but a few years later steam power was substituted. The first trial with this railway was made in March, 1826, in taking out a brig-rigged vessel that was successfully done, and shortly after several other vessels were taken out for repairs. The first use of the diving bell in this country is believed to have been made for cutting off the wooden piles for the outer end of these ways. This railway was built under a patent granted to John Thomas, a naval constructor,

This dry dock company was the first to build a tow-boat for that special duty. The towing of sail vessels in New York harbor and bay had been performed prior to 1825 by small passenger steamboats during the dull seasons, or when put out of business by new and more suitable vessels for some established route. On account of this marine railway being so far uptown at that date, it was necessary for the patronage of the several lines of packet ships and other vessels that were berthed in the lower part of the city, to have some means of bringing them to the railway for inspection and repairs, so the company had a small steam towboat constructed by Smith & Demon in 1828 and named "Rufus W. King." She was 102'x19'x7' and fitted with one of James P. Allaire's crosshead engines of 34 inches cylinder by 4 feet stroke. She was a queer-looking craft, having a square stern like a sloop and a bow as round as a full moon. She had very little freeboard, setting very low in the water. They burned wood in the furnace of the boiler to raise steam for propulsion, and under ordinary conditions her power was so small she could with difficulty tow a large vessel. At a later date she was disposed of and did general towing, and about 1847 the hull was lengthened, made deeper, and a larger engine put in the vessel and named "Buffalo:" she was then placed in the passenger service on the Hudson river as an opposition boat and was always in evidence when there was a steamboat war of rates.

Commander John Rodgers, U. S. N., President Board of Naval Commissioners, proposed in 1821 an inclined plane and dry dock "for building, preserving and repairing ships of war," and in fact constructed an experimental set of ways at the Washington Navy Yard upon which the 44-gun frigate "Potomac" of 1,700 tons, was hauled out of the water in 1822, and he says the experiment "fully confirmed his anticipations, and the ship was hauled up with comparative ease and perfect safety." Com. Rodgers proposed to the Secretary of the Navy that the subject of the adoption of the inclined plane with a house for the protection of the vessel from the weather, and the dry dock so-called, for the use of the navy department, be submitted to the President, which was done in January 1823, but it seems to have been lost sight of in the political game by Congress. Its advantages over the heaving down process were thus mentioned: "In the United States we have no docks: nor have we any way for preparing our ships for repair, but by heaving them down, a process tedious, very expensive, and highly dangerous, particularly to large ships, which are always in a greater or lesser degree injured by it. Nor is it possible to place a vessel hove down, in such a situation as to enable the mechanics employed in her repair, to work on her to the best advantage: much time will unavoidably be lost. The advantages and economy of docks, upon the principle of this invention in repairing ships when compared with the ordinary mode in the United States of heaving down are innumerable. The vessel can be taken into dock with perfect ease and safety, and there placed in the position most favorable for her thorough examination and repair from her keel up. Every facility to a minute examination and repair and every advantage to the mechanics in performing their work is afforded. Putting aside the risks and the loss of time in heaving down it may be safely stated that the labor of repairing in a dock of this description would be at least one-third less than the labor of repairing a vessel hove down."

This appears to be the last for many years of the inclined marine railway for government work, as the dry dock had the call at the time and the speculative contractor was getting in his fine work with Congress for a large contract, though it was several years before one was built.

That the marine railway and floating dry docks of the period were not all that were required, is seen from the fact that the New York Marine Dry Dock Company was incorporated by the New York Legislature in 1834, having as incorporators David Brown and Jacob Bell, shipbuilders; Captain Cobb, shipmaster; O. Mauran, shipowner, and E. K. Collins, shipping merchant and agent of a packet line, for the purpose of building a dry dock. Capital stock of the company was $250,000. It was proposed to be built of wood and located in a convenient place in the city between two piers for protection from injury, and to be sunk to a sufficient depth so that the top was two feet above the highest spring tides, and freed from water by a steam engine placed on one of the piers. The project does not appear to have been taken up by the capitalist, as there has been no record left of anything further being done by the company, except inviting subscription for stock of the company.

The increasing number of immigrants arriving at this port from Europe and the large increase in our Southern coastwise commerce made it necessary for the packet companies to increase the number and size of their vessels still further, and this brought an increase of business to the local shipyards. There were built at these shipyards during 1826 twenty-three ships, three brigs, forty-nine schooners, sixty-eight sloops, twelve steamboats, fifteen towboats and nineteen canal boats, making a total of 29,137 tons.

It was just about the time the United States Supreme Court gave its decision regarding the monopoly with steam vessels on the waters of the United States, and that our capitalists were taking measures to invest in steamboat enterprises, that a large fire in a New York shipyard took place, that was known for many years as the "Shipyard Fire." There was another fire in a city shipyard about twenty years later that was a very great loss, but this one was even greater. It occurred on March 14, 1824, about five o'clock in the morning, being discovered in the steam sawmill of Noah Brown on Manhattan Island, and spread with such rapidity that the mill and large ship house of Brown & Bell, just adjoining, were destroyed before any assistance could be rendered. In the ship house were two steamboats; one the "Hudson," being built for R. M. Livingston, nearly completed and ready to launch, and in the yard two brigs almost finished, besides a large quantity of ship timber, all of which shared the same fate. The flames also extended to the adjoining yard of Isaac Webb & Co., where a frame building belonging to Henry Eckford and occupied as a saw pit, and considerable quantity of ship timber was consumed. An effort was made to launch the steamboat, but the flames spread so rapidly that the workmen were driven from the ways and they had to abandon the attempt to save the vessel. Fire Engine No. 33, "Black Joke," that had been located at the lower end of the dock, as a point of great advantage to fight the flames, was cut off from the shore end of the yard by the sudden spread of the fire, and before the firemen could take any measures to remove their engine from its peril, it took fire and was entirely consumed. Several of the firemen were caught between the fire engine and the end of the dock, and their choice lay between the fire on one side and the river on the other; four of them jumped overboard, but were at once rescued by boats from the shore.* This fire was the cause of the formation of a noted fire engine company of New York City in the early days, Live Oak No. 44, organized August 2, 1824, by several of the shipbuilders around Manhattan Island, and was located in a house in the square at Houston near Columbia street in later years. Fire companies in these early days were not models of thorough organization. Being volunteer companies, there was a great deal of freedom given the members in the active operations of the company, and this brought out a feeling of rivalry between the several companies that very often when in fire service they came in collision, and a free fight was the result between the members of the different companies.

*Loss estimated at forty thousand dollars, Brown & Bell losing about one-half that amount.

Live Oak was able to "hold up their end of the plank" on such occasions.

The earliest claim to a ship model of a vessel is that made by Orlando B. Merrill of Newburyport, Mass., for one he made in 1796. The designer and maker of this model was engaged in shipbuilding from 1791 with his two brothers for several years, and was one of the most prosperous builders of that section at the time. He was one of the two contractors who built the U. S. sloop of war "Wasp," of 509 tons, in 1813 at Newburyport. This model is now in the possession of the New York Historical Society, having been presented to the society by David Ogden, the New York agent of the St. George's line of New York and Liverpool packets, and one of the original owners of the clipper ship "Dreadnought." On the backboard to which the model is fastened is the inscription: "Original ship model made by Orlando B. Merrill of Belleville, Newburyport, Mass., 1796, and by the inventor, now 90 years of age, given to David Ogden in February, 1853, who presented it to the New York Historical Society in 1853." This model is made in four pieces of a fine wood, and the form is far ahead of anything of its kind that we have left to us from that period. It is in a good state of preservation, and shows the surface of the wood is in its original condition. This model is 19¾ in. extreme length, 2⅞ in. in half breadth, and 2½ in. deep center of length. Of the shipbuilders in New York and vicinity there was a claim made for a model made by Christian Bergh, assisted by William Vincent, both shipbuilders in early part of the 19th century. Stephen Smith of Smith & Demon also claimed the credit for the early ship model. There is a model in Webb's Academy and Home for Shipbuilders showing the marks of having passed through fire. It is 44 inches long, 10 inches wide and 6 inches deep at midlength, and built up of six layers of hard wood. The form shows it to have been an old time model. The descriptive card on the model says: "Relic of model rescued from the ruins of the office of William H. Webb burned in the year 1848. This model was made by Isaac Webb, father of William H. Webb, about the year 1816 in the City of New York or its vicinity. It was the first model made in ships showing water lines, and rendering it much more easy to form the model and measure its shape than by the method used in all countries heretofore. The use of this method of modeling saved very much time, produced more beautiful vessels than formerly, and revolutionized the business of building sea going vessels in all maritime countries."

In 1830 there were fourteen shipyards that extended from just below Corlears Hook to Fourth street. There were also 244 journeymen ship carpenters, besides apprentices not yet out of their term of service, the caulkers, of whom there were not many so named, and the ship joiners, in all about 400 men. There were also some subcontractors having small shops or yards for repair work. There were also the sawyers and shipsmiths. It was at this period that some of the members of the old firms retired altogether from the business, or an active participation in the industry, and were succeeded by some of the younger men who were interested. It was then that so many experiments were made in the form of vessels, as well as in the motive power. The old spoon-shaped bow on the steam vessels was giving way to an easier entrance line, and a finer run aft, and many a steamboat was built at this period that was in service not more than one season than she would be taken out on the ways for alterations in her form suggested by the season's work. From 1830 to 1840 there was probably more experiments and alterations made on steam vessels in New York waters than in any other decade in the building of our merchant marine. They gained much knowledge at that time that was of service in later years. Robert L. Stevens, of Hoboken, N. J., did probably more toward improving the form of steam vessels at the time, through his experiments, than any other builder or owner of steam vessels. He had false bows built on some of his river steamboats as experiments, of varying lengths from the stem proper, securely fastened to the hull of the vessel, and built up for two or three feet above the water line. This was a steamboat era; but the changes had a marked influence upon the form of our sailing vessels. It was during this time that the first coastwise steam line was established between New York and Charleston, S. C., with a class of vessels not fitted for outside service. They were all built at New York, and named "David Brown," "Home," "William Gibbons," "Columbia," "New York" and "Neptune." When this steamboat era first opened about 1825 there were many who became interested in the business of steam navigation who had a limited amount of capital at their command, and had invested in vessels that were ill adapted for the business in which they were placed, and as competition in a few years became more active, such vessels were a losing speculation and their owners were in many cases forced to the wall, financially. By 1830 a weeding-out process took place, and the financially strong owners were found in possession of the higher class of vessels and the better paying business. Then began, again, the formation of stock companies, not the first, for Fulton & Livingston Company was known as the North River Steamboat Company, and with this the laying aside of the old type of steamboats, and experiments to improve the hull and motive power of every new vessel. They were now progressing toward another period of a greater and more radical departure in shipbuilding in this city and country. We see more of it in the shipyards of New York, for the Hudson River and Long Island Sound were the greater channels of travel prior to 1850 than any other waters in the United States, and as most all the vessels in service on the routes from New York were built in that city, its effect was naturally felt in the local shipyards. All the shipbuilding on the Atlantic Coast was not done at New York, for there were extensive plants on the coasts of Maine and Massachusetts that launched every year a large tonnage, mainly of sailing vessels. There were two yards opened in 1834 that were subsequently widely known for the steam vessels built there: Bishop & Simonson, foot of Walnut street, as builders of the "Lexington" in 1835 and many steamships: and William H. Brown as builder of Hudson River steamboats and steamships.*

Besides the improved type of steam vessels constructed at New York just prior to 1840, there was an improved type of packet ship placed in service for the American companies to accommodate the increasing passenger travel. The ship "Independence," built by Smith & Demon in 1831, of 732 tons, 140'x32'x16', had a reputation for several years for a high average of speed in her voyages in the European trade. The "Ajax," built in New York in 1832, is thus mentioned as a very superior packet ship: "In the gentlemen's cabin there are twelve berths, and in the ladies' six berths, all very spacious and furnished on the most approved plan of taste and comfort. The ceiling being about 8½ feet high, and the great breadth of beam renders the cabin altogether a very commodious apartment. The work is all bird's eye maple, satinwood, rosewood, caracas wood and mahogany. The pillars of the staterooms are all of the Corinthian order. Though some of our packets can accommodate a larger number of passengers, yet none of them surpass the 'Ajax' in neatness and comfort."

As the number and size of vessels had increased so largely, the inventive faculty of the American mechanic had been brought into play to devise some means to take a vessel out of the water for inspection or repairs to the immersed portion of the vessel, besides the means then

*The last vessel built by Noah Brown was the ferryboat "Sussex" for the New York and Jersey City Ferry Company in 1833.

employed on the marine railway, that had its objections. The New York Screw Dock Company began the operation of a screw dock in a slip between Market and Pike streets in September, 1827, the company being incorporated April 21, 1828. This dock, which was the first of its design, is thus spoken of by an engineer of that period: "The vessel to be raised by this apparatus was floated over a platform of wood sunk to the depth of about ten feet below the surface of the water, and suspended from a strongly built wooden frame work by 16 iron screws 4½ inches in diameter. This platform has several shores on its surface, which were brought to bear equally on the vessel's bottom, to prevent her from canting over on being raised out of the water. About thirty men were employed in working this apparatus, who, by the combined power of the lever, wheel, pinion and screw, succeeded in the course of half an hour in raising the platform loaded with a vessel of 200 tons burden to the surface of the water, where she remained high and dry, suspended between the wooden frames. At Baltimore I saw a large screw dock constructed on the same principles, on which the platform for supporting the vessel was suspended by forty screws of about five inches in diameter." There was a few years later a hydraulic dock built for Ring & Co., shipwrights, and located in the same vicinity, a portion of the mechanism of this dock having been constructed by Watt & Boulton, steam engine builders of Soho, England, and was fitted to raise a vessel of 800 tons. The perpendicular lift of this dock was ten feet. The first vessel raised was the ship "Great Britain" of 724 tons in June, 1835. After being secured in the dock she was raised out of the water in forty-five minutes. The mode of raising a vessel on this dock was to bring the vessel in between the two wharfs exactly over the cradle; the chains were then tightened so as to make the blocks come in contact with the keel; water was then forced into the cylinder through a small tube by means of a pump, which caused the ram to be forced out, drawing with it the sliding beams, raising the cradle with the vessel in a slow but steady manner, to the required height. The New York Sectional Dock Company had built a sectional dock from plans of Phineas Burgess and Daniel Dodge in 1839. This company was incorporated as the New York Floating Dry Dock Company on April 18, 1843, having a capital of $100,000. This dock was located in the vicinity of the other floating docks on the East River. To show that there was business for an increase of floating dry docks in the city at this time, it is found that there was in 1836 72 steamboats in service to and from New York that were built in the city, not including ferryboats or tugboats, the greater number having been built within three years.

The marine interests of New York were fully awake to the situation of ocean steam navigation long prior to any action in building vessels for the purpose in this country, for in 1839 there were two acts passed by the New York Legislature incorporating the Ocean Steam Packet Company and the North American Steam Navigation Company. The incorporators of the first named company were Charles H. Russell, Samuel B. Ruggles, W. H. Aspinwall, John Ward and William Kent. The incorporators of the last named company were William C. Redfield, Henry Grinnell, Robert Benson, William Kemble, Robert Carnly and John Griffith. These persons were well known in those days in marine circles in New York City. Nothing further appears to have been done at the time than the creation of the companies.

## TOOLS.

Prior to the separation of the colonies from the mother country, and no doubt for years later, some of the edged tools used in the shipyards were imported from Great Britain, and in many cases they were made by the local blacksmiths. There were attempts made in the

New England States during the 18th century to establish factories for making edge tools, though there is no record that they were of shipbuilding specialties, but they were of short duration. In 1806 there were in this city 40 "ironmongers and hardwaremen," but it was not until 1816 that Lewis Seymour opened a hardware store with mechanics' tools in Chatham street, and in 1824 Charles Merrill in Grand near Lewis street, that many of the older ship carpenters will remember, and who catered to the shipbuilding trade. There is one other who was in the center of the shipyard district at the time, and whose store was the center for the hardware trade of the shipbuilders, and that was William Wright, who opened in 1832 at North (or Houston) and Lewis street, known as Wright's corner. He was succeeded by Daniel D. Wright in 1840, who continued the business for many years.

When the first edged tools for ship carpenters, such as the broad axe, adze, slicer, maul, etc., as an established factory product was made, cannot be ascertained at this late day. When the country began to prosper after the 1812-14 war, and the packet lines were established for the immigration service, Congress began to wake up to the necessity of protecting still further some of the industries of the country, and then it was we find there were some earnest endeavors made to manufacture edge tools for home consumption, but it was not until about 1824 when there were three factories in New York State making axes and edge tools, scythes, etc.; but in 1826 the Collins Company was established at Hartford, Conn., making edge tools, with other steel and iron goods, and are still in active operation. There followed them in a few years Daniel Simmons of Cohoes, N. Y., and L. and I. T. White at Buffalo, N. Y.; who first made ship carpenters' specialties of these manufacturers, cannot be told. It was not until this period that the manufacturers ground the dull edges of the tools. By 1845 there were many manufacturers catering to this trade through New York State and the New England States, and the dealers in these specialties in New York City were numerous. It was during this period so many improvements were made in hand tools of all descriptions. There is no doubt the initial improvement in edge tools came about like several other changes in manufactures of the period, through the system of manufacturers brought to this country by the skilled labor from Europe about 1830, and the American mechanic, "knowing a good thing when he sees it," adopted some of the foreign practice in connection with his own, and even improved on that.

The first manufacturer of edge tools in New York City, with ship carpenters' tools as a specialty, was John Conger. He opened a small blacksmith shop in 1814 in Suffolk street, but in 1818 he branched out in making edge tools while located in Grand street. This was the period when prosperity was abroad in the country. He continued in the business at different places until 1845, when he closed up while located at 33 Attorney street. He was the pioneer edge tool manufacturer of New York City. William Horton, who had served his apprenticeship with John Conger, opened a shop in Fifth street near Lewis in 1837, and removed to Lewis street near Fifth street in 1840; was succeeded by Horton & Arnold in 1853, who remained on the old site until 1868: Samuel B. Arnold had been an employee of William Horton. About 1841 Lewis Watts and James M. Sheffield, who had also been in the employ of William Horton, started in the same line of business in Avenue D, and these two manufacturers had the monopoly of their line of business in New York City until about 1852, when W. S. Hawkins, who had a large blacksmith shop in Third street, near the shipyards, commenced the manufacture of edge tools in the same locality as the other manufacturers. This was during the period when all trades allied to shipbuilding were driven to the top notch. These manufacturers all went out of business after the close of the War of the Rebellion, on account of the shipyards being unemployed.

# CHAPTER IV.

## STRIKES OF SHIPYARD EMPLOYEES, AND FORMATION OF TRADE UNIONS IN NEW YORK CITY.

HE subject of the relations between skilled labor and the employer in New York City in the early days has never been fully written on account of the scarcity of material, but such data as is available at this day show us that the New York Journeymen Shipwrights' Society was the first labor association organized in New York City. The constitution for the government of this society is dated January 5, 1804, and contains the names of forty-eight of its members. The fee of initiation for the first six months after the foundation of the society was one dollar, for the second six months two dollars, for the third six months three dollars, and to the end of four years four dollars, after which it was five dollars initiation fee. The monthly dues were fifty cents a month. One provision of the constitution stated that "This society shall be composed of the shipwrights and caulkers residing in the City and County of New York." It became incorporated by an act of the New York Legislature on April 3, 1807, as the New York Society Journeymen Shipwrights. The purpose of the society was shown in the provision in its charter, where it says: "In order to raise a fund for the support of such of the members of said society as may by means of sickness, lameness, age or other causes become unable to labor." The United Benevolent Society of Tailors of the City of New York was incorporated April 12, 1819. The Cartmen's Benevolent Society of the City of New York was incorporated January 28, 1820, and the New York House Carpenters' Architectural and Benevolent Association was incorporated March 14, 1826. One provision of its charter says: "That the members of this incorporation shall not at any meeting of said corporation pass any resolve, motion, by-law, rule, or regulation, which shall in any manner control or fix the price of carpenters' wages in the City of New York, or shall restrain any member from receiving or paying wages as he or they may deem proper." The Shipwrights' Society of 1807 in all probability ceased to exist prior to the expiration of its charter. There was another society composed of the mechanics of that trade at a later date, that was not incorporated, a certificate of one of its members being now at Webb's Academy and Home for Shipbuilders. This certificate was of "The Union Society of Shipwrights and Caulkers of the City of New York did on the 11th day of November in the year 1824 admit Hezekiah Webb as one of their members for life. John Lozier, Prest., Nehemiah Waterbury, Sec'y." This Hezekiah Webb was a ship carpenter residing at this time near the Manhattan Island shipyards. All of these societies were formed for beneficial purposes, without any idea of a combination in an industrial sense as a trade union. Mutual benefit societies of the various classes of mechanics and tradesmen for mutual assistance appear to have been a prominent feature in the social organizations of the cities during the first decade of the 19th century. Philadelphia was the city of most importance in this line, for the record shows that most of these associations were incorporated, and included the Carpenters' Society, the oldest, organized in 1724; the Shipmasters, Pilots and Mariners' Society; Stonecutters' Company; Master Bricklayers' Society; Hair Dresser and Surgeon Barbers' Society; Typographical Society; Master Tailors' Society; Provident Society of House Carpenters; Master Mechanics' Benevolent Society, and similar societies of the cordwainers, journeymen blacksmiths, journeymen tailors, who had two mutual benefit societies, and journeymen hatters, bricklayers and coopers, and a society of master coopers.

It had been the custom in the shipyards, as of all the various trades, for the mechanics to labor from sunrise to sunset, but about 1825 there began to arrive in this city a few immigrants who were skilled mechanics of the different trades, mainly from Great Britain and Germany, and a few of these were ship carpenters. The industrial depression and many strikes at this period in Europe was one cause of this heavy tide of emigration of skilled machanics and others to this country, who hoped to obtain more and better employment at their trades. Prior to 1830 there began to be agitated in the city shipyards the subject of the long hours of labor, and for a few years this subject was one that engaged much attention. The American mechanic had been brought up to believe that work from sunrise to sunset for a major portion of the year was his portion in life, even though he might consider the hours too long; it was a part of his early education. All those who were willing and able worked as long as they could see by daylight, masters, journeymen and apprentices, storekeepers, professional men, and where possible into the night; they all did it. It was the habit and custom that had been handed down to that generation. It was when the foreign mechanic and laborer had arrived in numbers on these shores, and taken time to spread his radical ideas of the rights of labor, with socialistic reform, free love, community of interests and some other 'isms, the last four repudiated by almost the whole native mechanic circle, that the American mechanic began to view the labor question from a different standpoint, and then began the further agitation of the relations of labor and capital that in a few years assumed such large proportions, sooner than if the native mechanic had been left to work out his own salvation from a condition that was almost slavery. The issue was only forced a few years earlier to a crisis than if the native mechanic had been left to his own resources. It was through the social and political complications then taking form, that the Native American party, a political organization that was a factor in our politics for several years, was formed.

As we come to view at this later day the situation of the American mechanic when these imported social reform theories were placed before them, we can have an idea of what must have been their opinion of them. To have one of these radical reform theories to digest at a time, was as much political economy as our social conditions could at that time make room for; but to have five or six of them, and all on different lines, turned loose on the American public at about the same time, and for them not to have been carried away by much of their sophistry, shows the stability of the American people, and particularly the native mechanic, as clearly demonstrated under somewhat similar conditions of later years. They do not take kindly to that kind of reasoning.

The educational advantages of New York City at this period were of a very inferior order. The free schools of the city were attended by only the children of the very lower order of society, while the native skilled labor, tradesmen and middle class patronized the private schools of which there were about four hundred and fifty, the former being generally classed as charity schools. This had been the case for many years.

To a workman in a shipyard during these days life consisted simply of the abundance of hard work, with a little rest and fairly good nourishment by way of variety. Much recreation was almost out of the question on account of the exhaustion from such long continued day of toil. The writer was told by a shipbuilder who was an apprentice for Smith & Demon prior to 1830 that many evenings he has come home from the yard so completely worn out physically from the labor of the day, that he has laid down to rest, fallen asleep, too tired to eat his evening meal. This was not once, but many times.

The more this question of long hours was agitated the more burdensome it became to those who were obliged to labor under its rules. It was continued for more than two years with frequent small strikes at a few shipyards, but the men having no common plan among them for their guidance, they made little progress at the time. It was the first stage of an industrial crisis in this country, and they lacked an intelligent guiding hand. Some of these strikes were partially successful, but most of them were failures, so they did not command much attention at the time. The workmen of the shipyards were not the only mechanics that were now agitating the labor question to better their condition of employment. It was general among the various trades in our large cities, and was manipulated in the City of New York by the scheming politicians to their own advantage for a time.

The shipyard employees applied for a reduction in the hours of labor, but were each time met with a refusal. They were no more unfavorably situated in that regard than were the other trades workmen at the time. The shipbuilders had resolutely set their faces against any reduction in the hours of labor, more especially those who had taken contracts based on the old time hours of labor, who saw that a change in the hours would mean a loss to them in the completion of their contracts. Thus the contest was fought step by step, without any material gain by either side. It was a period of education for all those interested in more ways than one. What added to the life of this agitation, and became a great aid to the public discussion of this question, was the establishment of low-priced daily papers in our large cities, that came within the means of the laboring classes, and that catered to the interests of their patrons. A few of these papers are still published, the New York Herald and

The Sun.* There were several labor journals started at the time but they were all short lived. It seems remarkable that copies of these papers cannot be found.

The step that eventually brought the question of the hours of labor to a settlement in the shipyards was the incorporation of the New York Journeymen Shipwrights' and Caulkers' Benevolent Society on April 9, 1833. There had been since the mechanics' bell was first erected in 1831 a more general agitation of the subject by the employees, and through this means they were brought more closely together, which resulted in the organization of the society in 1833. This brought a more harmonious and united organization, having a common purpose, and under better leadership, to wage the battle for shorter hours with the builders. The opposing interests were now making ready for the final stand in the long drawn out conflict. This was succeeded after many conferences, between the builders and the employees, by the latter giving their ultimatum of ten hours for a day's labor, the builders having offered increased pay for the old hours of labor, but this the employees refused. The builders finally gave way to the inevitable, having seen the handwriting on the wall. This was some time in 1834, from which time can be dated the termination of the first successful agitation for a ten-hour day by a trade organization of mechanics in this country. This was what led to the more general and permanent recognition of the mechanics' bell. It was rung at 6 a. m. to begin work, 8 a. m. for breakfast, 9 a. m. for work again, 12 m., 1 p. m. and 6 p. m. to cease work for the day. When it is brought to mind that each yard was equipped for the time-honored custom of ringing a bell to announce the hours of labor in the yard, that was to govern all those employed there, it will be seen what a radical departure had

*Prior to this the "blanket" sheets having a limited amount of reading matter and selling at three cents a copy, and over, were the only daily journals in the city; of value to the politician, and the shipping merchant.

been taken by the employees in dictating the hours of labor, and in sounding forth those hours in the day to all interested through their own instrument. The operation of this bell was the means of doing more at this period, in all the mechanical industries in New York City, far beyond its sound, than any other agent to break down the long hours of labor, that had been handed down by custom for so many years. The shipbuilders had their early business training under those long hours, and they considered this the proper time for a man to labor. But fifteen years had brought many changes. The American mechanics of that period had more educational advantages than those of earlier days. Foreign labor had now entered the field at a time the native element was considering the question of throwing off the chains of long hours, and through efforts of all working for a common end the ten-hour system was obtained by all the trades eventually.*

One of the features in showing how far personal interest can be carried under different surrounding conditions, was seen during this agitation by the shipyard employees, where a few of the latter were most enthusiastic in holding forth the claims for a reduction of the hours as well as an increase in the wage scale, and were always ready to express their views on the then prominent question of the day in industrial circles; but when they were operating a shipyard of their own at a later period, and during a large strike when they had several unfinished vessels on the stocks, were most bitter opponents of labor interests, and contributed their share to the defeat of the strike at the time. They were not in the "band wagon" of industrial progress at this time. They were no longer labor leaders; they were now one of the "capitalistic"

*There is no evidence that there was any concert of action between the New York shipyard employees and the trade unions during the strike period. The former evidently carried on their struggle independent of other labor organizations.

class, and protecting their interest on the inside of the fence.

### TRADE UNIONS OF NEW YORK CITY.

The trade unions of this period in New York City were a result of the large immigration from Europe during the period under review. From Great Britain alone, and this includes Ireland, there were over 80,000 emigrants that arrived at New York between 1825 and 1830, but not all of this number remained in the city, for the means of communication from New York to the Western States were improving very largely every year. Large numbers were going West to follow agricultural pursuits, while others were engaged for work upon new railroads just started, and public improvements in near by States, while many who brought their tools of trade with them remained in the city. These people had left Europe when trade unions were under investigation, for combinations even for securing higher wages or shorter hours was held to be criminal under the common law, and those taking part in such action were liable to criminal prosecution. Strikes were frequent and long continued in England at this period, and that was one reason for so many coming to this country at the time.

By 1829 the many theories of social reform and political economy began to be very prominent through lectures and discussions in the daily journals, and it was not very long before a workingmen's party was organized in New York City having many of these imported theories in its platform. This gave the leaders of the old political parties considerable anxiety for a time, but they soon got in their "fine work" inside the organization, and in less than two years by internal dissensions the organization went to pieces. The American mechanic, as a class, would not endorse such theories, but the politicians used it for all it was worth to them.

The developments of the time showed that organization of the trades workmen was taking form, but it would seem that no trade unions were formed in the city until 1833, on account of a slight depression in business and later by an epidemic of cholera in New York City in 1832, when business was very generally suspended for several months. These trade unions were organizations without being incorporated, as there is no record to be found in any of the State or city public offices of record of such organizations of that period. The unions formed in 1833 consisted partly of the tailors, masons, hatters, saddlers, coopers, printers, cordwainers or shoemakers, piano makers, cabinet makers, curriers, weavers and carpenters. There were others no doubt. These unions were controlled by the General Trade Union, organized the same year and composed of delegates from the several trade organizations, and was the first labor federation or league in New York City.

This General Trade Union exerted much influence on the several trade unions, and its officers during the early days of the organization were: Ely Moore, president, politician, printer; Henry Walton, vice-president; James McBeath, recording secretary, bookbinder; John H. Bowie, corresponding secretary, currier; Robert Townsend, junior treasurer, carpenter. We see that a politician, who had held office under the city government, had the office of power in the organization, but this came through a political upheaval in the city at the time, with the Equal Rights party coming to the front. The president of the organization made an address before the General Trade Union in December, 1833, that gives us some light how the relations of labor and capital were held at that time by the labor interests. The speaker was a representative of labor in the front ranks at the time, and a few extracts from the address will be of interest. "We have assembled on the present occasion for the purpose of publicly proclaiming the motive which induced us to organize a general union of the various trades and arts in this city and its vicinity, as well as to defend the course, and to vindicate the measures we design to pursue. We conceive it to be a truth enforced and illustrated by the concurrent testimony of history and daily observation, that man is disposed to avail himself of the possessions and services of his fellow man without rendering an equivalent, and to prefer claims to that which of right belongs to another. This may be considered a hard saying; but we have only to turn our eyes inward and examine ourselves in order to admit to the full extent the truth of the proposition, that man by nature is selfish and aristocratic. * * * Wherever man exists, under whatever form of government, or whatever be the structure or organization of society, this principle of his nature, selfishness, will appear, operating either for evil or for good. * * * Much, however, can be done toward restraining it within proper limits, by unity of purpose and concert of action on the part of the producing classes. To contribute toward the achievement of this great end is one of the objects of the General Trade Union.

"Wealth, we all know, constitutes the aristocracy of this country. Happily no distinctions are known among us save what wealth and worth confer. No legal barriers are erected to protect exclusive privileges or unmerited rank. * * * The greatest danger therefore which threatens the stability of our government and the liberty of the people is an undue accumulation and distribution of wealth. And I do conceive that real danger is to be apprehended from this source notwithstanding that tendency to distribution which naturally grows out of the character of our statutes of conveyance, of inheritance, and descent of property, but by securing to the producing classes a fair, certain, and equitable compensation for their toil and skill, we insure a more just and equal distribution of wealth than can ever be effected by statutory law. Unlike the septennial reversion of the Jews, or the

Agrarian law of Rome, the principle for which we contend holds out to individuals proper motives for exertion and enterprise. We ask then what better means can be devised for promoting a more equal distribution of wealth than for the producing classes to claim, and by virtue of union and concert, secure, their claims to their respective portions? And why should not those who have the toil, have the enjoyment also? Or, why should the sweat that flows from the brow of the laborer be converted into a source of revenue for the support of the crafty or the indolent? I am aware that the charge of illegal combination is raised against us. The cry is as senseless as it is stale and unprofitable. Why, I would inquire, have not journeymen the same right to ask their own price for their own property, or services, that employers have, or that merchants, physicians, or lawyers have? Is that equal justice which makes it an offense for journeymen to combine for the purpose of maintaining their present prices, or raising their wages, while employers may combine with impunity for the purpose of lowering them? I admit that such is the common law. All will agree, however, that it is neither wise, just nor politic, and that it is directly opposed to the spirit and genius of our free institutions, and ought therefore to be abrogated."

There were no aggressive steps taken now for some time that were called to public attention, probably for the reason that they were feeling the pulse of the employer on the question of hours and scale of wages. The first trouble of any magnitude appears to have broken out between the master tailors and the journeymen tailors in February, 1836. The latter refused to work for an employer who failed to keep a slate hung up in a public part of his store, on which should be entered the name of every journeyman taking work from his store. And that workmen should not take a job out of their turn as laid down by the association: and that the members must refuse to work for less than the union rates. The contest was carried on for several weeks with spirit and energy on both sides, and very often with violence on the part of the strikers that called for the intervention of the peace officers of the city. The guardians of the peace of the city at this time consisted of watchmen who did the night service, and were called "Leatherheads" from the imitation of a fireman's hat they wore. They were supposed to keep the disturbing element of the city under control, but the latter had little respect for their brief authority, or their clubs. There were also a small force of constables who did duty at the courts and day service in the city. This was a force not exceeding 500 officers for a population of 200,000. In February "the mayor ordered the militia on duty. The bands of foreigners, instigated by the mischievous councils of the trades unions, and other combinations of discontented men, are acquiring strength and importance which will ere long be difficult to quell." These strikers became so encouraged by their freedom from arrest for their disturbances, and they carried their strike on such lines as to show an utter disregard for the public peace, that it became necessary to arrest several of the strikers. These men were brought to trial in May, 1836, and twenty-one of them were convicted of conspiracy and riot, and each one fined from fifty to one hundred and fifty dollars, according to his prominence in the trouble.

The charge of Judge Edwards of the Court of Oyer and Terminer in the sentence of the prisoners gives a still different view of this labor question at the time. "Your case affords a striking manifestation of the necessity of the law extending its protection to the individual aimed at. The object of your combination was not only to control the merchant tailor, but even the journeymen. Your rules were craftily devised to accomplish this object by throwing out of employment any master or journeyman who would not submit to your dictation. But you were not content to stop here. You appointed committees to act as spies upon those whom you wished to subject to your will. Then premises were placed day and night under their vigilant inspection. You thronged around their shops and were guilty of gross acts of indecency. The journeymen who took jobs were followed to their dwellings and otherwise annoyed by you. In short, every ingenious devise was resorted to by this extensive combination to which you were attached, to effect your object. Associations of this description are of recent origin in this country. * * * Judging from what we have witnessed within the last year, we should be led to the conclusion that the trades of the country which contribute immeasurably to its wealth, and upon which the prosperity of a most valuable portion of the community hinges, is rapidly passing from the control of the supreme power of the State into the hands of private societies, a state of things which would be as prejudicial in its consequences to the journeymen as it is to the employers, and all who have occasion for the fruits of their labor. * * * They are of foreign origin, and I am led to believe, are mainly upheld by foreigners."

To show how a part of the labor community had been affected by the conviction of the journeymen tailors and to what extent class hatred was carried, is shown by the posting of a placard around the city which contained within the representation of a coffin the following words:

"THE RICH against THE POOR."

"Judge Edwards, the tool of the Aristocracy, against the People. Mechanics and Workingmen, a deadly blow has been struck at your Liberty. The prize for which your fathers fought has been robbed from you. The freemen of the North are now on a level with the slaves of the South, with no other privileges than laboring, that drones may fatten on your life blood. Twenty of your brethren have been found guilty of presuming to resist a reduction of their wages: and Judge Edwards has charged an American jury, and agreeably to that charge they have established the precedent that workingmen have no right to regulate the price of labor: or in other words, the Rich are the only judges of the wants of the Poor man. On Monday, June 6, 1836, these freemen are to receive their sentence, to gratify the hellish appetites of the Aristocracy. On Monday the liberty of the workingmen will be interred. Judge Edwards is to chant the Requim. GO, GO, every freeman, every workingman, and hear the hollow and the melancholy sound of the earth on the Coffin of Equality. Let the courtroom, the city hall, yea, the whole park be filled with mourners. But remember, offer no violence to Judge Edwards. Bend meekly, and receive the chains wherewith you are to be bound. Keep the peace. Above all things keep the peace."

This was not the only strike, but was no doubt a test case forced into prominence by the General Trades Union at a time when they thought they were sufficiently strong in numbers and influence in the city, and with enough political backing to force the issue to a successful termination. The only occasion when this body of delegates came forward to publicly support the action of the unions was on this occasion, when they issued a notice of their endorsement of the action of the trade union, in part, as follows: "At a special meeting of the delegates of the Trades Unions of New York and vicinity on Friday evening, February 12th, the following Preamble and resolutions were adopted: *Whereas*, a combination of men styling themselves the Master Tailors have through various newspapers declared that they will not receive into their employ any man who is a member of the U. T. Society of Journeymen Tailors of this city. *We, the delegates* of the different trades in convention assembled considering that by the above avowal of proscription these said masters are arrogantly attempting to coerce the independent spirited men who have taken upon themselves the unquestionable right of affixing a value of their own labor." After going into the subject more generally, they conclude their resolutions with "*Resolved*, that this convention recommend the different societies attached to this union, to take the preparatory steps as soon as convenient to ensure additional means to support the United Society of Journeymen Tailors while on the strike. *Resolved*, that the corresponding secretary of this union be instructed to open immediate correspondence with the different unions of the United States apprising said unions of the struggle of the Journeyman Tailors."

There was another condition surrounding the labor question at this period that had a marked effect upon the laboring classes, and this was the matter of slavery in New York State. This was permitted to exist until the New York legislature in 1817 passed an act that there should be no slavery in the State after July 4, 1827, when ten thousand slaves were set free by this act. It was to the former slave owners in the Northern States, as well as those of the Southern States that the labor leaders hurled the name of Aristocracy. Included in the same class, in the State of New York, were many men who had a hold upon the dominant political party in the State, who for some years had made a practice of obtaining charters for incorporated companies, and covering among other things, charters for banks and specialties in industrial pursuits. These men had accumulated wealth through the disposal of these special privileges, and their course of action had been noticed by the industrial classes with marked disapproval. This was a scandal that did not die out in a short time. Were our forefathers free from graft in business?

Ely Moore, who has been brought into notice as the first president of the General Trades Union in 1833, was in the next year elected as the Workingmen's candidate from New York City to the House of Representatives, where he took his seat in December 1835. He was the only representative of the labor interest in Congress at that momentous period. There was already sufficient political friction between the two sections of the Union, with the question of finance and the slavery question to discuss. But to stir the Aristocracy into opposition still further, the claims of labor must be thrown into the arena of debate in our national hall of legislation. The only extended speech on the labor question Congressman Moore made was on April 28, 1836, in reply to some references made by Southern members of the House to the labor question during a debate on the Army Appropriation bill, in which he said, in part: "Having been long and intimately connected with their cause, and approving as I do of their principles and measures, I cannot consent to hear them assailed without making an effort to vindicate them. They have been denounced as Agrarians, Levelers, and Anarchists, and their union as unlawful and mischievous. * * * The honorable gentleman in the course of his remarks holds the following language: I entreat, gentlemen, to look well to the consequences of the experiment of sending the government there (to the North) as a competitor in the labor market, and under the constraint of positive orders to expend this vast sum, let labor rise ever so high. It is already one dollar a day, when in the South and West it is only fifty cents. These appropriations are not for this year alone. They are the beginning of a system of lavish expenditure which will last until 1842, no longer; my word for it. Are the judicious men of the North, the property holders of the North, disposed to organize in their bosom this army of day laborers, men, who all over the world, spend between Saturday and Monday the wages of the week, and who at the period of their disbandment in 1842 will be penniless and who must go supperless to bed, unless they rob by lawless insurrection or by the equally terrible process of the ballot box? Let gentlemen look at it.

They are in quite as much danger of insurrection as we are." The laboring classes, the backbone of the democracy of the country rob through the ballot boxes? What are we to understand by this? * * * That none but the wealthy ought to be allowed to vote, and that the minority should govern. * * * Let this doctrine be carried out, and the principles upon which the government is founded are utterly subverted. * * * I regret the attack has been made. It may lead to a controversy from which it will be most difficult to exclude jealousies, heart burnings nad recriminations. I am not quite certain, however, that it will not in the main be productive of good. It may serve to establish more distinctly and more permanently the landmarks which distinguish the two great political parties of this country—the Democracy and the Aristocracy. * * * It is idle to attempt to disguise the fact, that the time is coming and now is, when the political gulf between these two parties must be widened and deepened. * * * It was with regret that I heard such sentiments uttered. It was with regret that I heard the integrity of the laboring classes so unjustly impugned, and if it shall be the last act of my life I will attempt to hurl back the imputations. I fear that those attacks upon the people, which have become so common of late, are a prelude to a premeditated assault upon popular freedom. Public violence and disorder, generally, if not universally, have their origin in a violation of the principles of equality and justice, and when these principles are outraged, it is generally by the few and not by the many, it being the manifest interest of the majority to preserve them pure and unimpaired. All the horrors, enormities and abominations consequent upon the French revolution had their origin in the oppressions practiced by the aristocratical few. But much has been said against associations. Not of bankers, nor of brokers, but of mechanics and laborers. Why, it has been asked with alarm and indignation, why this commotion among the laboring classes? Why this banding together and forming of unions throughout the country? These associations are intended as counterpoises against capital whenever it shall attempt to exert an unlawful or undue influence. They are a *measure of self defence and of self preservation*, and therefore not illegal. Both the laws of God and Man *justify resistance* to the robber and homicide even unto death. They are considered necessary guards against the encroachments of mercenary ambition, tyranny, and the friends of exclusive privileges therefore may with propriety dread their power and their influence. The union of the working man is not only a shield of defense against hostile combinations, but also a weapon of attack that will be successfully wielded against the oppressive measures of a corrupt and despotic Aristocracy. The present indications of disquietude on the public mind excites no alarm among the friends of Equal Rights. It is a proof that liberty is abroad, and that "the bone and muscle of the country" are imbued with its spirit. And who are they that clamor against the efforts of the laboring classes to protect their rights and elevate their condition? Who that approve of indictments and prosecutions against them, for seeking refuge in union and association from combination and oppression, and hold guiltless at the same time the confederates of all conspiracies against them? I will tell you who they are: they are the sordid champions of exclusive privileges and of chartered monopolies, those cunningly devised substitutes of feudal tenures, and the insolvent prerogative of primogeniture. They are the common enemies of equal rights, and of that just and benign policy which would secure the greatest good to the greatest number. They are the Aristocracy, and therefore traitors to the principles of the government which affords them protection."

The journeymen tailors were not the only trade union in New York City at this period making demands for recognition of their rights and of their organization. The shoe manufacturers, having their business in this city and their plants in New Jersey, were at this time tied up with strikes of the operatives, who in some instances would go to as extreme lengths as the other organizations under similar conditions. The Morrocco Manufacturers of New York City, Brooklyn and Newark, N. J., were at this time under the ban of the Leather Dressers' Trade Union Association, composed to an extent of imported labor, where they claimed "that the trade union is an impenetrable rampart to the Aristocracy of the country, and a shield to the workingman from the aggression of capital on the rights of labor: that we individually and collectively pledge ourselves to maintain and support the union."

It is a fact patent to all, that during the early stages of this trade union period in particular, and undoubtedly later, there were many men who became connected with the several organizations, and with the main body, who had no interest in common with the supporters of the union, who were unprincipled and unscrupulous, bound to the organization by ties of working the thing for all it was worth." Grafters, we call them at this day, and some of that stripe have been sent to the State hotel at Sing Sing by the Courts of New York for a stated period of late years.

Again it must be borne in mind that many of the members of these trade unions were those with but a limited education, and in some cases none at all: and it was a struggle for existence, for sustenance for themselves and families, without much hope to raise themselves far above their low estate. This was the class of people who by placing much confidence in the hands of these schemers, were very often used by the "grafters" for their own purposes. The less educated and more inexperienced officers of the trade unions very often abused their powers of the organization in their dealings with the employers. There was a total want of a peace making policy, no policy at all, no tact, nothing but brute force very often displayed by both sides in the contest. Here is what I offer you, take it or that is all you will get. That is the spirit that was manifested, and is it any wonder the employers combined for their mutual interest against such demands; or that the laborers rebelled? This led to a feeling of resentment on both sides, though for business reasons may have been subdued for the time being, and did not die out for many, many long months.

The trade unions and the frequent strikes when they were pressed into action by those who were active in such work, walking delegates, or business agents they are now called, came to an end without any outward sign, and seemed to gradually melt away. When the surrounding conditions are taken into consideration it is not strange that the whole movement went up into the air. The decisions of the courts on the labor question no doubt had a marked effect for one reason. The latter part of 1836 saw this strike fever dying out, a presidential election was then on the way, and in a few months the business panic of 1837 had brought on a stagnation in the industries that threw very many of the laboring classes on their own resources, and the trade unions were left without support by the members, and as the leaders did not see a very promising field of labor for the near future, dropped the whole thing, and the organization fell from the want of support. When business revived again during the following year most of the trade unions had ceased to exist, and wages of mechanics were at a lower level than they had been for a long time. The supply of skilled labor was greater than the demand. This ended the first trade union fever in this country, and it was many years before it broke out again.

The first change to the ten-hour system in government service appears to have been under an executive order of President Van Buren of March 31, 1840 * * * "hereby directs that all such persons, whether laborers or mechanics, be required to work only the number of hours prescribed by the ten-hour system."

# CHAPTER V.

## MECHANICS' BELL.

HERE are some features surrounding the original mechanics bell that were not made clear until they were brought out through an examination of the permit from the city authorities for the erection of the tower supporting the bell. On September 5, 1831, at a meeting of the Board of Aldermen "A petition of Isaac Hadden and others for permission to place a bell on the vacant square at Manhattan Market was read and referred to the Aldermen and Assistant Aldermen and street commissioner." On September 12 following, the official papers say that "The Alderman and Assistant Alderman of the 11th Ward, and Street Commissioner, to whom was referred the petition of a number of persons for the privilege of erecting a bell frame in the square around Manhattan Market, presented the following report in favor of the same: 'The Alderman and Assistant Alderman of the 11th ward, and Street Commissioner to whom was referred the petition of shipsmiths, carpenters, etc., who work at the different shipyards at or near Manhattan Island, praying permission to erect a sufficient frame or fixture in the vacant space around Manhattan Market, on which to suspend a bell for the purpose of giving regular notice when to commence and when to quit work, beg leave to report: That on examination they find the petitioners have procured a sufficient bell for the purpose, that there is abundance of room in the vacant space referred to to erect a frame or small enclosure without incommoding the public or any individual, and your committee deeming it proper to grant the prayer of the petitioners, respectfully offer for the adoption of the Common

Council the following resolution: Resolved, if the Board of Assistant Alderman concur, that James Dobbs, Isaac Hadden and associates be permitted at their own expense, under the direction of the Superintendent of Wharves, to erect in the northwestern corner of the square around Manhattan Market a sufficient frame and enclosure on which to suspend a bell, provided that the

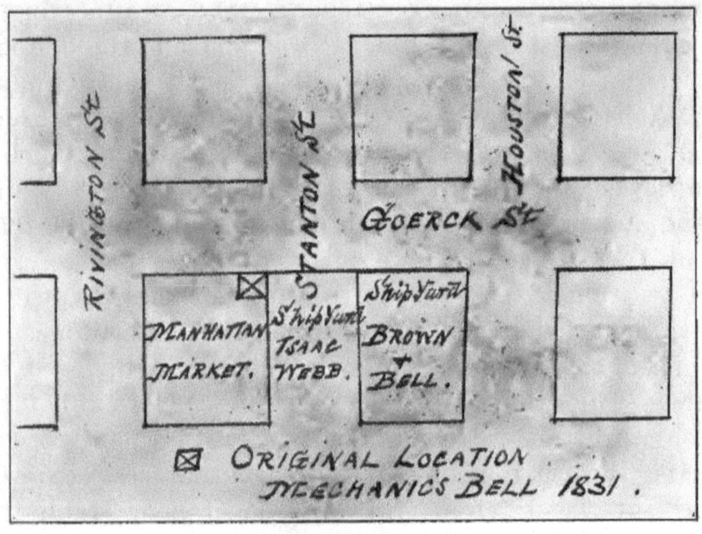


said frame or enclosure shall not exceed 10 square feet (?) at its base, be handsomely finished, painted, and kept in repair, and that the said frame and enclosure, and bell be removed from off the premises whenever the Common Council shall direct, by resolution or otherwise, provided that the corporation may cause it to be rung at fires.' " This report was approved by the Board of Aldermen, and sent to the Board of Assistant Aldermen for concurrence. The Market committee of the Assistant Board of Aldermen on September 19th following reported "on petition of sundry persons to have permssion to erect a bell frame in the square around the Manhattan

Market, granting the same. Concurred in." This completes the official record showing that the privilege to erect a bell tower on city property had been given on September 19, 1831.

The two representatives of the petitioners to the city authorities were James Dobbs, a ship carpenter, and Isaac Hadden, a spar maker.

It has been a matter of some thought to those who have given the subject a study, why the original bell was located so far up town, when the greater number of shipyards were below Grand street, for at this time there were only three shipyards above Grand street: these were Isaac Webb & Co., Brown and Bell, and Smith, Demon & Comstock, the latter being at foot Fourth street.

In the report of the committee of the Board of Aldermen is found a few words that show this bell was erected by a comparatively few shipyard employees, and was a matter that concerned only a certain locality. It says: "the petition of shipsmiths, carpenters, etc., who work at the different shipyards, at or near Manhattan Island." This clearly shows that the employees of the yards of Webb and Allen, Brown and Bell, and Smith, Demon & Comstock, had associated themselves together for the purpose of making a custom of the ten-hour system of work, irrespective of their fellow laborers in the other yards in the city. There was at this time a want of unanimity, that had been growing for some time, among the employees of the different yards as to the proper course to pursue to obtain their object of ten hours a day. This came from the fact that these shipyards at and near Manhattan Island were occupied by builders who were the latest, and largely patronized by the owners of steam vessels, more so, probably, than the builders situated at Corlears Hook, and the employees at the former yards come to look upon the structures launched from the Manhattan Island yards as being the finest production of the shipbuilders art in the city, which bred in their minds the opinion that the building of steam vessels was a higher branch of the business than the construction of sailing vessels. This produced something of a feeling between the employees at the two localities, and while it was not carried so far as to break off all intercourse between the employees at the different yards, it left a strained feeling between them that prevented any united action being taken for the good of the whole number, and at the same time caused a want of confidence on both sides that remainded for about two years. It has been considered by some who were employed in the yards at that period, that the builders so manipulated affairs as to bring the labor interests in the shipyards of the two localities in opposition to one another, thinking by so doing that there would be no unity of action taken by the men during the then period of labor agitation, and fostered this feeling until it became a want of confidence on both sides, and so continued to keep them from any united action until the formation of the society in 1833, when the builders' labor troubles ended. The location of this original bell at Manhattan market square thus became the action of a portion of the shipyard employees of the city at the time, and was established as a local affair through the want of unity among those most interested.

This original bell could not have been of a large size, for the restrictions placed upon the dimensions of the tower in which the bell was to be hung, were, "that the said frame or enclosure shall not exceed ten square feet at its base." (Should this be ten *feet square?*) Taking into consideration that the bells in the fire alarm towers in the city at this time, with the exception of the City Hall bell, were not over thirty inches diameter at the mouth, it is fair to say that the original mechanics' bell, with its small tower compared to the fire alarm towers, was about eighteen inches diameter at the mouth and was operated by a rope. A bell of this size would have been of little service in that location to the employees of the shipyards at Corlears Hook, that were located about one half a mile further down the river, with rising ground between the two locations. This bell did service in the same tower until 1834 or 1835 when a larger bell was erected in its place, and *it may* have been one of the small bells from the fire alarm towers that were now being changed for those of larger size. It is thought by some of the older shipyard employees at this day that the original bell was recast with additional metal. This bell remained on the same tower, that was about twenty or twenty-five feet high, and sent forth its notes to many a joyful mechanic calling to mind his relief from the long hours of labor each day, such as his forefathers were compelled to perform. By 1844 the shipyards extended in an almost solid line along the East river from Grand street to 12th street, with a few still at Corlears Hook. The location of the industry had so greatly changed from the time of the original location of the bell that it was now considered advisable to place it in a more central location, and with that purpose in view it was removed in that year to a vacant lot southwest corner of Lewis and 5th streets, and in view of some differences with the owner of the lot who was a shipbuilder, the shipyard employees, who were the owners of the bell and structure, removed them a year or so later to Bishop & Simonson's yards nearly opposite* Here it remained and did working day service until 1872 when the whole affair was removed to foot of Fourth street. At this time there was not one shipyard on the New York side of the river that was open: the few that were in active operation were at Williamsburg and Greenpoint, and they were few, and not heavily burdened with work. The bell still was kept in operation. In the early part of 1880 it became cracked, and it was necessary to have another one take its place,

*It was now rung by a rod fastened to a lever, that was operated similar to a pump handle.

MECHANICS' BELL 1845.

so a new bell was cast from the metal of the old one by James Gregory of Cannon street, the brass founder, who had been in that location since about 1850, being the successor of William Buckley, the bell founder. This new bell remained in the same location, and the cause for its operation having passed away, it was removed on February 10, 1897, to Webbs Academy and Home for Shipbuilders, where it is expected to remain undisturbed as one of the few remaining relics of New York's old time shipyards. There has been a proposition made to have the bell erected in a tower such as it occupied in its days of activity, on the grounds of the Academy at Fordham Heights. This bell is 36 inches diameter outside at the mouth, 26½ inches high, and 20 inches at the crown and weighs about 900 pounds. There is cast on the body of the bell, Mechanics Bell—Gregory—New York 1880.

# CHAPTER VI.

NEW ERA IN SHIPBUILDING—OCEAN STEAMSHIPS—FIRST CLIPPER SHIPS.

THERE now arrived one of the most important epochs in the industrial development of this country: no more in other mechanical pursuits than in the shipbuilding industry: and what is of interest to all citizens of New York City is the fact that this city contributed its full share of the progress in the arts and sciences of the time, and never flagged in its endeavor to keep up with the march of industrial progress in this country. Our renowned sailing packets had a few years before met competition in the European trade by steam vessels of foreign companies, and for a time the packets were able to hold their own in the passenger trade. In a few years these vessels were succeeded by sailing vessels of a sharper model. Younger men had in many instances come into control of the older yards. New yards had also been opened, and more progressive ideas were again taking hold of the shipbuilding business in the city, and in a few years the beneficial effects of these changes became apparent. The packets had been increasing in dimensions for ten years or more, so that by 1840 those under construction were near to 1,000 tons each. This type of vessel, with the full bow and wide square stern was the fast sailer from 1816 to 1840, but after the latter date there developed various branches of trade in which a quick delivery was as important for trade purposes as it was for the passenger trade. The restless energy of the American merchant began to show again in our foreign commerce. For instance there was the tea and spice trade from China and East Indies to the United States, in which a short time delivery had always been considered of much importance. The cargoes consisted of tea, coffee, dried fruit, etc., which were liable to deteriorate in a voyage of four months or more to the home port, and to shorten the voyage as much as possible was desirable for many reasons. The first tea clipper ships were the "Helena," built in 1841 by W. H. Webb, then the "Montauk" by the same builder, and the "Rainbow" by Smith & Demon in 1844, and the "Houqua" in the same year by Brown & Bell, the "Sea Witch" in 1846 by Smith & Demon, and the "Samuel Russell" in 1847 by Brown & Bell. These vessels were not representative of the clippers of a few years later: they were much smaller, and the early ones were not so heavily constructed so as to stand the whip and spur for driving as were those of later years, though some made remarkably fast voyages, and passed through some trying occasions at sea.

It must not be thought that our packet ships, catering to the emigrant passenger trade on the Atlantic ocean, mainly with Great Britain, were making long voyages at this time, for there were several then running to New York after 1840 that made voyages from New York to Liverpool in 16 days, and from Liverpool to New York in 22 days. The average for one year was 23 days from New York to Liverpool, and 34 days from Liverpool to New York. These were all New York built vessels.

The system of construction of the larger vessels was not always the same at the different periods. Up to about 1830 the skilled mechanic in the shipyard performed work of any character that was necessary to the building of the vessel. He would aid in the hewing out to the lines, the frames of the vessel, and participate in setting them up in their proper places. Would line out his strake of planking on the timbers of the vessel, dub off the outer surface of the frames so that the plank might fit truly: put on the plank, bore the holes for the treenails and bolts, fasten the plank in place, and even caulk the seams of the planking: and when it became necessary to have a large and heavy stick of timber placed in position in the vessel, all hands were called from their work to carry on their shoulders these large pieces of timber, sometimes taking twenty-five or more men. After the ten hour system was brought into practice there was a breaking up of the labor in the yards, each man having a specialty, as a carpenter, caulker, fastener, etc., the men in each kind of work called a gang. This change took some time before it came generally into use, but it was a system under which time was saved and better work secured than under the old system. Subsequently derricks were installed at the better yards for handling the heavy timber, and some yards never made improvements in methods of building unless forced to do so. Treenails were at first made by hand, and were chopped out of sticks of wood with axes: but a treenail lathe machine was invented in 1838 to do this work more quickly and accurately.

A later view of the question of labor in the shipyards has been obtained by an examination of the payroll of one of the largest of our old-time New York shipbuilders, that runs from 1840 to 1845. It is found that in 1840 the ship carpenters were paid $2.00 per day, and the caulkers the same daily wage. This rate continued for the better class of mechanics for near ten years. The apprentices, of which there were six in this yard at the time, were paid from 50 cents to 64 cents per day, according to their length of service and their skill. A year later this yard had for its skilled labor 13 ship carpenters and 18 caulkers, and a few months later the number of carpenters had increased to 26 and there were ten apprentices. In the summer of 1842 there were 79 ship carpenters employed on seven sailing vessels and one steamboat. Among the apprentices now employed here, some of whom had been for a greater time than others employed in this yard, may be named those who were well known in the business at a later date as men of known skill in shipbuilding at New York: Eckford Webb, a brother of W. H. Webb, George Bell, these two subsequently became partners in business at Greenpoint, L. I.: George Wilmurt and Leonard Bolles. They received now from 50 cents to 78 cents per day. There were now eight sub-contractors, or lumpers so called, at work in the yard on eight vessels. In May, 1843, there were eight vessels under construction at one time, with twelve carpenters and fifteen apprentices, and eight sub-contractors. In September 1844 there were ten vessels under construction at one time. Christian Metzgar was the foreman at this yard during the whole period of its activity.

The shipyards of 1840 to 1845 were somewhat changed in location from what they were a decade before. There were now but few yards, not more than four, at Corlears Hook, a new one being established in 1841 by Westervelt and Mackey, who in 1844 moved their yard to Lewis and Seventh street. This firm was of much prominence during the later years of prosperity. It is found that the shipyards extended in almost a solid line from Grand street to Twelfth street, where William H. Brown had for a few years been building vessels. William H. Webb was then located at Sixth street, Smith and Demon at Fourth street, and Brown and Bell at Stanton street. William H. Brown and John English were now in control of the marine railway at Tenth street, and had most of the repair work on vessels of large tonnage in the city. Some of the other builders, besides those previously named, on the New York side of the river, were Jabez Williams, Devine Burtis & Co., Haythorn & Steers, Bishop & Simonson, Buckman and Casilear, Whitlock and Berrian, Bayles & Brown, William Bennett, and Lawrence & Sneeden.

The building of the first clipper ships had no more than got well under way than great improvements were made in the new steamboats put under contract: they

STEAMBOAT "OREGON," BUILT BY SMITH & DEMON.

were of larger dimensions, more commodious, having staterooms and more propelling power of machinery. These vessels were now for the large transportation companies mainly, though there were a few for individual owners. A few years later there began inquiries regarding the building of steamships for European service, and later it assumed the form of a postal contract with the United States Government, and in 1847 when a company had been organized Westervelt & Mackay were given the contract for building the first American ocean mail steamships. This was followed the same year by William H. Webb building the "United States" for Charles H. Marshall & Co. of the Black Ball line of packets: and in 1849 Westervelt & Mackay constructed two for the Havre line. This completes the list of ocean steamships built prior to the far-famed Collins line of steamships. The fleet of this company were the "Atlantic" and the "Arctic," built by William H. Brown, and the "Pacific" and the "Baltic" by Brown & Bell, and the "Adriatic," or at first intended to be named, the "Antarctic," by George Steers. About the same time began the building of the steamships for the Southern coastwise lines, the "Northerner" for the Charleston line in 1847, the "Falcon" in 1848 for the California trade, both by William H. Brown; the "Georgia" in 1849 by Smith & Demon, and the "Ohio" by Jeremiah Simonson in the same year, both for the California trade. In the same year the first steamship for the Savannah line, the "Cherokee" was built by William H. Webb. There were a large number of steamships built during this period for service occasioned by the gold excitement in California. This latter factor added immensely to the business of the New York shipyards, as it did to the shipbuilding industry of other Atlantic coast cities, both for steam vessels as well as for sail vessels, that lasted for four or more years. The extension of our coastwise commerce with steam vessels at this period was a factor of much interest to the local shipyards, as the larger number of these vessels were built at New York. Then to increase the business still further there was a lively competition going on between the several established lines and outside interests on the Hudson river, and the demand for four or more years was very great for high speed passenger steamboats of large size, several of which made long runs on the river in record time that is even of interest at this day, and all of them built at New York. So we see there was a steady hum of the broad axe in our shipyards not many years prior to its first stage of decline.

Referring to the high speed steamboats of the Hudson river, built during this period of intense rivalry on the river at New York City shipyards, it will be of interest to refer to some incidents in the career of the "Empire," built by William H. Brown in 1843, and the

"Thomas Powell" by Lawrence & Sneeden in 1846, vessels that were well known on the river at the time. The facts referred to are those lately published in the Scientific American Supplement in a series of papers by the writer on "The Development of Armored War Vessels and Armor Plating in the United States," where he says:

"What gave our naval architects, as well as Col. Ellet, the first practical demonstration of the value of the principles of high speed and strength of a vessel to destroy an enemy's vessel by forcible contact was that of the occasion of a light-built river steamboat running into a solid-built pier in the City of New York, with comparative slight injury to the vessel. It was in the early morning of April 25, 1845, that the steamboat 'Empire of Troy,' of the New York and Troy line was coming down the Hudson river, and when opposite the upper part of New York City during a fog on the river, ran into the end pier of the new dock at 19th street, about thirty feet from the outer end, and cut her way through the timbers of the dock and stone filling of the cribwork. This pier of cribwork was 40 feet square. There were three of these piers under this dock, the latter being 265 feet long from the bulkhead and 40 feet wide, and lacked the heavy plank facing to be completed. The sills, string pieces, and heavy timbers of the dock were of rough timber 18 inches square, and the 'Empire' cut through these with a 'tremendous crash,' cutting them short off, as a light piece of wood would be cut with a sharp tool. These timbers were afterward found to be sound and free from defects, excepting those caused by the steamboat collision. The 'Empire' plowed her way through the solid rock filling of the pier some 27 feet before stopping. The opening by measurement at the time showed the 18 inches of timber, then solid stone filling of 8½ feet thick, and then through earth and rubbish 17 feet further, making a total opening of 27 feet long, and 17 feet deep at the deepest point. The stem piece of the vessel was carried away, several of the forward ends of the planking on either side were badly shattered, and a few of the frames started. Both of the forward ends of the hog frames of the vessel were broken.

"When the type of vessel is taken into consideration, being 307 feet long, 30 feet 6 inches beam, or about 1 to 10, and built with a flat floor that ran well out to the fore body of the vessel, to make her as light draft as possible; coming down the river with a strong tide, that was on the last hour of the ebb; and when the filling of the pier was the most exposed, it is certainly remarkable that the vessel was not more seriously injured; but as it was, the hog frames being partially broken and otherwise badly strained, showed the vessel received at the time a severe shock throughout the whole structure. It was only that the vessel was traveling at a high velocity when she struck the pier that saved her from being badly crushed, for it must be remembered she was not a heavy-built vessel, nor was she a shell. She was undoubtedly moving at the time of the impact at not less than 12 miles an hour. She had been racing all night from Albany with an opposition boat, and the time made from Albany to the pier when struck showed an average of 18 miles an hour. This was no accident.

"This ramming incident was variously commented on at the time by those in the more progressive marine circles, and it caused much speculation and thought on the subject of steam vessels being brought into forcible contact at a high speed. It was a subject of much local comment for some time how the vessel escaped destruction.

"There was one other incident of the same nature that occurred some years later, and these complete the list of wooden-hull river steamboats running into stone crib piers with slight injury to the vessel, in the United

States. The 'Thomas Powell' was running between New York and Catskill on the Hudson river as a night boat, and on July 23, 1868, when about four miles from her berth at the former city, ran into a dock at the foot of 59th street, North River, and met with comparatively slight damage when considering the age of the vessel. It seems that the vessel ran into a thick fog during the night on her trip down the river. The pilot on watch in the early morning had but a limited experience on steamboats, though he had seen several years' service on the river. He was feeling his way down the river in the fog, and up to four o'clock, when the vessel ran into the dock, had been making a speed of about 12 miles an hour. The vessel struck the string piece of the dock with a fearful crash, and this was the first warning they had of the impending danger. Some idea of the velocity of the vessel when striking the dock may be formed, when stating that she tore diagonally through the superstructure of the dock between two piers of stone cribwork, and forced her way through until the paddle wheels struck the cribwork, and she did not bring up or stop her progress until about one-half of her length was laid on the pier, and the ends of the vessel hanging over the sides of the cribwork. Her port water wheel was badly damaged, its shaft forced two feet aft from its proper position, with the crank pin and main pillow block broken. There were one or two planks started on the port side, but not of sufficient damage to take her out on the drydock. The vessel was relieved from her dangerous situation at the next flood tide. The dock had been damaged by ice two years before this occurrence, and was partly overflowed at high water. The tidal conditions at New York this morning were low water at 5 a. m., so the vessel was running with a favorable ebb tide, and it was on the last hour of that tide when she struck the pier. This vessel was 231 feet long originally, and it is believed she was lengthened a few feet when staterooms were added, drew about six feet of water, and was twenty-two years old at the time. Her main shaft was located about 95 feet aft of the stem of the vessel. Taking into consideration the age of the vessel, and the manner of her striking the cribwork at such an angle as to bring all the strain on the port side of the vessel, it is a wonder that she was not irreparably damaged. It proved that she was still a sound and strong river vessel, even with her years of service. She was employed on the river until 1881, when retired after thirty-five years of service. There were material differences between these two cases that no doubt affected the result. The 'Empire' was a new vessel, and ran into a dock that was just about completed. The 'Thomas Powell' was then twenty-two years old, although in as good condition as any wooden vessel of her age: and ran into a dock that had been built for several years, and was then in a partly dismantled condition. What the result would have been had the vessel struck a more substantial pier under similar conditions is very problematical."

The first steamships built at New York, if not in the United States, were the "Lion" and the "Eagle" in 1841 by Jacob Bell for the Spanish government. This takes no account of the "Robert Fulton" of 1819. The next year William H. Brown built for the Russian government the "Kamschatka," a side wheel vessel of over 200 feet long for naval purposes. Then followed our domestic vessels just noted. Up to and including 1850 there had been constructed at New York 38 steamships: William H. Brown building nine, William H. Webb building eight, Westervelt & Mackay building eight, Jacob Bell, Jeremiah Simonson, Thomas Collyer, Smith & Demon and Perrine, Patterson & Stack the remainder.

The only other fire in a New York shipyard that was considered of much moment after that at Adam & Noah Brown's yard in 1824, was one that occurred at William H. Webb's yard on April 8, 1848, about ten o'clock at night. It started in a stable next to the office of the yard that was located on Lewis street near 6th street. The flames spread rapidly from several points, and before the fire department could become active on the scene the flames had spread to the adjoining mold loft and the office, the former containing many old and valuable patterns and molds, and several historically valuable models. The fire also extended through its close proximity in the buildings to the Steamship "Panama" then on the stocks and nearly ready for launching in a few days, that was somewhat damaged, and required some rebuilding of a minor character before it was ready to launch. The fire department had to use great efforts on this vessel to save it from entire destruction, being ably assisted by the many employees of the several ship-yards in the vicinity who had come at the first call. There was also a large quantity of valuable timber that was lying near the vessel, some finished and some unfinished, and intended to be used on vessels then under construc-

CLIPPER SHIP "CHALLENGE."
Built by William H. Webb 1851.

tion in the yard, that was destroyed by the flames. The books and papers in the office were mostly all saved from the flames. The fire was believed to have been the work of an incendiary. During the fire a number of persons got on a workshed that covered the sawpit, to have a better view of the fire, and from the great weight on the roof the supports gave way, and all those on the roof were precipitated with a great crash of timbers into the sawpit below. Several persons had their limbs broken and others were more or less injured, and one died from internal injuries. This fire was the occasion when the owner of the shipyard was asked by one of the fire officials where the fire department could be of the most service at the time, and Mr. Webb told them, "if you can save my steam chest you will help me most."

The conditions existing at this period were the results of the many changes that had occurred in the last decade. Some of the shipbuilders had broken loose from the practice of the past, and taking lessons from their experience had made changes in the forms of their new vessels that were in many cases of much advantage to the owners. We must remember that at this period, though no more than at an earlier one, it was running counter to old customs to propose any radical changes, let alone to carry them into effect, in any business or profession even though it promised much improvement. There were those of our naval architects at this period who were in the front rank of their profession, and the general form of vessel they approved for a given service have been but little changed to this day. An English naval architect at this time said: "It seems now to be admitted in Europe and in America, that if a shipbuilder wished to have a very easy and fast going ship, he must give her bow not the round, convex line which was formerly adopted, but a fine, long, hollow line. In this consists the great revolution of the last twenty years. Formerly the broadest part of a vessel was one-third part from the bow: now it is one-third part from the stern. This is the principle on which the American and English clipper ships are built." The hollow entrance water lines were first used in this country by Robert L. Stevens in the early '30s, on his Hudson river steamboats. There were some of our well-known New York shipbuilders, so wedded to their old theories of design, that after 1850 they constructed clipper ships having the broadest part of the vessel one-third the length from the stem, like the old style packet ships, but with finer entrance lines.

By 1848 there was seen to be a demand for increased dry-dock facilities in this city for large vessels for repairs and inspection, caused by the larger vessels, both steam and sail, building at that time. The Balance Dry Dock was the patents of John S. Gilbert of New York of March 25 and May 12, 1840. The first dock built on this principle was a small one of 110 feet long by 45 feet wide in 1841, and was located at first on the west side of the

S. S. "ADRIATIC" ON BALANCE DRY DOCK.

city. The New York Balance Dock Company was incorporated April 18, 1848, and they had built a dock 210 feet long. The "Big" Balance Dry Dock was built by William H. Webb in Williamsburg in October, 1854. The principal dimensions were 325 feet long, 99 feet breadth, 38½ feet deep. There were twelve pumps operated by two horizontal engines, one on each side of dock, and two large locomotive boilers furnishing steam for the latter. "On each side of the dock, about six feet within the outer timbers, and extending from the bottom to top of dock, a very heavy and strong longitudinal truss or hog frame, formed of large uprights, top and and bottom chords and large iron bars crossing each other diagonally, the whole being strongly secured to the bottom of dock, cross trusses, diagonal braces, and top deck frame. This hog frame is planked on the inside, thus forming water tight tanks the whole length of the dock, on each side and bottom." This dock cost about $175,000 to build. The machinery was constructed by Mott & Ayres, machine builders of West 26th street, New York City, who built about the same period two or three iron hull steamboats for South America. This is the dry dock that was sold to the Erie Basin Dry Dock Company about 1890. In 1852 the United States Navy department had four floating dry docks, a balance dock of 350 feet long at Portsmouth navy yard, and a duplicate of this dock at the Pensacola navy yard, a sectional dock of 9 sections at the Philadelphia navy yard, and a sectional dock of 10 sections underway at San Francisco, Cal. There was a floating box dock to take up vessels of not more than 500 tons at Pittsburg, Pa., as early as 1831. This dock was fitted with four pumps that were operated by a steam engine. There were two of these docks at the same city in 1836.

The "heaving down" process is thus referred to by an authority as late as 1851: "The rapidity, safety and ease with which caulking and sheathing are now done contrasts strongly with the practice years since in vogue, and only completely discontinued within the last fifteen years, of heaving down vessels for this purpose by main force upon the beach occupying the space covered by our whole upper line of docks on the East river. This was performed at high water by fastening tackles from the head of a vessel mast, itself secured by heavy braces to heavy blocks and falls in the dock, until the keel of the vessel came out of the water, when on the succeeding tide she was thrown over. Previous to the construction of the United States Dry Docks even the largest government vessels were treated in the same rough manner."

# CHAPTER VII.

LAUNCHING OF VESSELS AND LAUNCHING DISASTERS — DRY DOCK ACCIDENTS.

HE launch of a large vessel, or of one constructed for some prominent transportation line, either a sailing vessel or a steam vessel, was sure to bring together at the shipyard a large number of people from all parts of the city, and from the immediate vicinity, to witness the launch, for an event of that kind was most always an item of news, especially in the later days, in our daily journals for a few days before the launch, and was always attended by many people as one of the free shows and entertainments of that period. After the successful launching of the vessel into her native element there was always a collation spread by the builders of the vessel then launched, in the mold-loft of the shipyard, where the invited guests of the builders, and those of the owners of the vessel, were invited to partake of their hospitality for the occasion. The employees of the yard were not forgotten on such occasions by their employer and the owners of the vessel, for their good work in the launching of the vessel was recognized by those directly interested in providing a bountiful supply of the substantial food of life topped off with rum punch, and freedom from work for the remainder of the day; and on some occasions a few of them would be incapable of further service at their daily labor for the remainder of the day, if it had been found necessary.

There has always been a great freedom from accidents in launching of vessels in this city, though the builders always knew there was an element of risk they must assume in taking a contract through the launching of the vessel. That the early builders had their trials, and it may be some accidents in launching their vessels is hardly to be doubted, but the record of them is missing. The first occasion where there was an error of judgment in the launching of a vessel seems to have been in April, 1842, when the ship "Union" of 133'x30'x19' built by Jabez Williams at foot 7th street for the New York and New Orleans trade, was launched full rigged, and just as she took an even keel in the water, careened over on her beam ends, in consequence of too small amount of ballast, under the launching conditions. She was soon righted without much injury, and at a small cost of repairs to the builders. There were a few similar cases to this in later years, but they did not attract much attention at the time. The most serious case that happened was that of the attempted launching of the ship "Sweepstakes," built by Westervelt & Mackay, of 216'x41'x22', on June 18, 1853, for the California trade. In sliding down the ways the vessel moved about half her length into the water when she suddenly stopped her onward movement, then careened over and struck the staging alongside and around the stern of the clipper ship "Kathay," then under construction in the yard, which broke down and precipitated a large number of spectators into the water, who had taken advantage of the choice situation for a good view of the launch, but they were all recovered during the excitement of the unusual occasion, without anything much more serious than a good ducking and fright. Steam tugs were at once brought into service to endeavor to pull the vessel from her awkward and dangerous situation, but so firmly imbedded was the vessel that all the hawsers used in the work were broken, as well as the timber heads in the vessel were torn out by the strain put upon them. They now resorted to the use of a floating derrick, fastening ropes around the stern of the vessel and to the derrick arm, thus taking up part of the strain the vessel was laboring under between the shore and the floating end. They propped the shore end up by blocking again to try and launch her at the next high tide, but were not successful in getting her off. Another floating derrick was added to give further relief to the vessel. She lay in this dangerous situation for about seventy-six hours, when a more than usual high tide, and the continual work that had been done under the shore end of vessel, brought relief to the vessel and she was safely set afloat. She was in a few days taken to the Brooklyn navy yard dry dock for inspection and coppering her bottom, where she remained for eight days. The vessel was badly strained in her top sides and joiner work, and it cost the builders all of twenty thousand dollars for the extra expenses of launching and repairs to the vessel. The cause was attributed by some to the sinking of the ground under the ways after the vessel had started her launching movement. In the light of further experience and a more close study of the conditions surrounding the launching of a vessel by our naval architects, it would seem as though this vessel was passing through the "tipping" process when the keel struck the shore, that had not been sufficiently cleaned between the ways. The vessel was brought up very suddenly and careened over against the vessel that was building at its side. The builders had been advised of the small clearance there would be for the keel of the vessel during the placing of the launching ways, but they thought "she will cut her way through," and took the chances.

It would seem from all human calculations that these builders had furnished their share of experiment and cost of repairs, for themselves and others to profit by for some time, in the accident to the "Sweepstakes." But not so: and in fact before the latter vessel had been completed after her launching, the vessel that lay alongside the "Sweepstakes" when launched, remained on the ways three or four days after the first effort to put her overboard. The clipper ship "Kathay" built for the California trade was to have been launched on August 11, 1853, but all efforts proved unavailing at the time in placing the vessel overboard. Powerful levers and jack screws were applied to the ways, but the vessel refused to move. The launching ways were relaid and the tallow renewed, and after the builder had been about eighty hours making endeavors to get the vessel afloat she was successfully launched. The extremely high temperature of the atmosphere had melted the tallow between the ways.

In the launching of the steamboat "New World" for the Peoples' line from New York to Albany in August, 1848, at William H. Brown's shipyard, owing to the improper placing of the ways and the effect of the high atmospheric temperature upon the tallow on the launching ways, the first efforts to launch the vessel were unavailing. The vessel moved about forty feet and then came to a stand, and all efforts to move her were ineffectual at the time, even with the services of the two tugboats. The smoke from the friction of the upper and lower ways told them one cause of the trouble. The vessel was blocked up, the ways relaid with a tallow mixture, and after fifty hours in that situation was at last successfully launched. Lawrence & Sneeden met with a similar experience in September, 1850, in trying to launch the steamship "North America" for the opposition line on the Pacific Ocean to California. The vessel was in a similar situation for about forty-eight hours before being placed overboard. The "ribbon" on the ways has sometimes given trouble in the launching of a vessel.

The whale ship "Niagara" of 700 tons, 130'x30'x18' built by Smith and Demon for owners at Fairhaven, Mass., was launched on July 30, 1851, careened over just as she left the ways, but was eventually hauled up to the dock and made fast, and righted by the use of block and fall similar to the heaving down process. There was not much damage done to the vessel. In April 1854, William

Perrine launched from his yard at Williamsburg the ship "Henry Harbeck" of 800 tons. The vessel went off the ways as any well disposed vessel should, but in consequence of ballast shifting in the vessel during its downward course on the ways, she careened over on her beam ends when fully afloat, and swinging around from the straight path of the ways struck an adjacent dock, carrying away a large portion of her main rail and shaking up the guests who were on board the vessel for the launch, with no broken bones but an abundance of fright for a time.

The "Big" Balance Dry Dock built by William H. Webb and finished in October, 1854, was not put afloat on the day set for launching, for when the blocks had been knocked away, and the structure bore its weight on the launching ways the dock refused to move. After blocking up the structure again preparations were made for rigging up battering rams and applying jack screws to the seventeen launching ways, and the next morning a vigorous application of these tools started the dock toward her natural element, and a successful launch of the dock was the result. Freezing of the tallow in the ways was not the cause of the trouble in this case, as the temperature of the air was not so low as to produce that result, the per cent. of grade to the launching ways being too low for the size of structure, and number of ways is considered to have been the cause.

The firm of Westervelt & Mackey was financially embarrassed about 1856, but the business was continued at the old yard by S. G. Bogert in their interest. They seem unfortunate in launching one of their vessels once more, for on April 8, 1857, the steamship "Queen of the Pacific" of 3,000 tons for Charles Morgan & Sons was hung up on the ways in consequence of the ways being of an insufficient length and improperly laid. The bilge of the vessel cut through the ground to such a depth after moving a portion of the distance that it held her fast on the ways. A sufficient quantity of earth was removed so that the vessel started again on the ways, but when not one half the length of the vessel was afloat she stopped her onward movement again. They now had to resort to extreme measure to extricate the vessel from her embarrassing situation. To get her afloat it became necessary to support the bow of the vessel with a boom derrick, clear the earth from around the keel into which it had settled, repair the ways and give them additional strength, and with jack screws to raise the after part of the vessel for blocking. With the use of jack screws and several tug boats they got the vessel afloat after being in that perilous situation for about 87 hours. This vessel never went into service for her original owner, but was sold about two years later to Commodore Vanderbilt and named "Ocean Queen."

Even the builders of later years are not free from such trials, for the steamer "Pilgrim" of the Fall River line, built by the Delaware River Iron and Shipbuilding Company was hung up on the ways after moving about 150 feet on July 13, 1882. Three attempts were then made to launch the vessel, but they were unsuccessful. The ways were then removed from their places, fresh tallow placed between them, and then put back in their proper places, and an extra set of ways placed under the bilges. An engine was also fitted and fastened on board the vessel and connected with anchors in the river to aid in starting the vessel, with four hydraulic pumps. With all this preparation it was more than a week after the intended launching before the vessel was overboard. From the high atmospheric temperature, the weight of the vessel had pressed out and burned the tallow from the ways.

While some of our American shipbuilders may think they have had the limit of trials placed in their hands at times, if they will look up the launching of the steamship "Daphne" in July, 1883, they will find a disaster that must have tried the builders to the limit, even though it may be said the design of the vessel had been condemned for some time. The vessel was built by Stephen & Sons of Glasgow, Scotland, and was 175'x25'x13'6", and when launched had not moved more than her own length from the shore when she careened over on her port side, and sank in less than three minutes, carrying down one hundred or more men to their death by drowning. Faulty design was given as the cause of the disaster.

Of accidents to vessels while in the dock for inspection and repair there have been but very few cases indeed considering the large number of vessels taken out of the water, and such cases as there is any record of is not more than three decades ago. The first was of the iron hull steamship "Crescent City" x "Massachusetts," while being raised in the sectional dock at foot of Clinton street on March 28, 1878. The dock had been raised not one half its required height, with the vessel in place to fully take the blocks at the proper time, when a crash came and the vessel listed over to the starboard side. The weight of the vessel fell with great force on the light frame structure of the upper work of the dock and crushed a large portion of one side. The vessel then slowly righted herself and fell to the portside. The dock slowly sank and left the vessel afloat. The next day the vessel was placed on a larger sectional dock, where she should have been placed at first, as the former was too small and light for a vessel of the dimensions of the "Crescent City." In October 1881, or more than three years later the same vessel went through a somewhat similar experience with the exception that in the first instance there were no persons injured, while in the second accident there was one man killed and two badly injured. This time the vessel was coming out of the dock, the structure having been sunk and the vessel floated, and while waiting for the tugs the tide had fallen so much that it was feared the keel of the vessel would touch the floor of the dock, and those in charge were apprehensive that she might under those conditions list over, so they started to pump up the dock and block up the vessel, and it was while this was being done that she careened over. As the tide rose the vessel righted and she was taken out of the dock without any further trouble. The dock was strained, but the vessel had but three or four large dents in her plating where she lay on some of the blocks.

The next mishapor accident wason the"Big"Balance dry dock on May 18, 1882, while taking up the steamboat "City of Boston" of the Norwich and New York Steamboat Company and was of a very serious character to the vessel. The vessel fell as the dock was being raised and its floor well cleared above the water. As it was unlike in many features any other case of which there appears any record, a few extracts from the judges' opinion in the case throws a flood of light on the details. "The boat was dismantled. Her walking beam was out; much of her engine was out of position, and the known object of having her raised upon the dock was to bolt down her engine keelsons. * * * The elevation of the boat from the floor of the dock called for by the contract was unusual. No boat of the size of the 'City of Boston' had ever before been blocked to such a height upon this, nor, as far as it appears, upon any other floating dock. The boat to be sufficiently elevated above the floor of the dock to enable bolts seven feet long to be passed up through the bottom and engine keelsons without being bent. * * * Instead of adopting this precaution known to be sufficient to remove all danger of falling, the defendants adopted a method of arranging the blocks necessarily involving a risk of the vessels falling, and endeavored to diminish the risk by 'dogging' the blocks, piled single and by, for the first time in the use of this dock, putting braces between the blocking. So far as the evidence discloses the decision to pile the blocks single was not arrived at because of any difficulty or expense attendant upon 'crib-

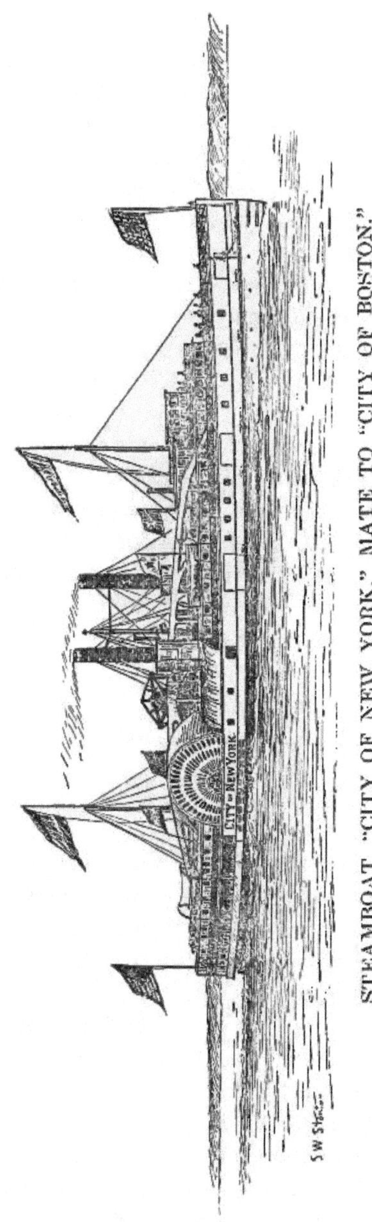


STEAMBOAT "CITY OF NEW YORK," MATE TO "CITY OF BOSTON."

bing' the blocks, nor because single blocking secured by dogs and braces was supposed to be more secure than cribbing. The only reason for the course pursued, suggested to me by the testimony is, that the cribbing would require a greater number of blocks than those at hand. But whether impelled by this or some better one, the fact remains, that between two methods of constructing the blocking open to be adopted the defendants chose the one involving risk, as against one that would have involved no risk. This was negligence, and the negligence that caused the disaster. * * * Upon the evidence the libellants are in no way responsible for the means which the defendants adopted to give the boat the requisite elevation from the floor of the dock. * * * After the 'City of Boston' fell she was raised by the defendants upon the dock with the blocks fore-and-aft cribbed, and then she was raised in safety. When the first attempt to raise her was made, however, the blocks were not cribbed, but placed one upon the other, single, until the requisite height was reached." It was proved that there was a sag in the dock, so that when raised it retained fifteen or twenty inches of water on the floor in the deepest part, to which the judge refers; and there was evidence tending to show that motion was imparted to this water upon the floor during the raising of the vessel. "I do not think the inference unwarranted that a jar was given to the dock sufficient to topple the boat over, as she was blocked, by some movement of the water upon the floor of the dock." The hull was so badly injured that it became necessary to put in very nearly a whole new bottom in the vessel, besides renew some joiner work that was pretty badly strained. The vessel was on the dock about five weeks after being raised the second time. A judgment was found against the dock company for $76,291.31 that some years later was settled for about $30,000. At the time of the disaster the current opinion in marine circles in the city was that the superintendent of repairs for the steamboat company and in charge of the work was responsible for the damage, but it is seen by the judges' opinion that those in charge of the dry dock were solely responsible.

A few years later a small balance dock lying at the foot 26th street, Brooklyn, in August, 1887, had taken up the bark "Maria Louise" of Palma in the Canary islands. This vessel careened over after having been raised several hours, without much warning. The dock took a list from one of the compartments springing a serious leak at night. The vessel received much damage and several of the crew of the vessel were badly injured.

The most serious accident in loss of life and injuries to persons, in this country at least, was that which befell the army transport "Ingalls" on June 14, 1901, while being taken up on a balance dock at Erie Basin, Brooklyn, where there were three lives lost and about fifteen injured, all being workmen employed on the vessel at the time. The vessel was almost out of the water when there was a crash, the vessel went over and with such momentum as to carry the dock over at the same time in a depth of water of thirty feet. There were eighty or one hundred men at work on the vessel at the time, and it is remarkable that more were not killed and injured than were accounted for. The dock was an old one, but thought to be in good repair, and of service for a vessel of the size of the "Ingalls." There was a weak spot in the dock, or improper blocking of the vessel that was never fully accounted for. Was there a sag in the dock, and collection of a body of water on the floor at the time, as in the case of the "City of Boston"? It has been referred to that the same expert foreman who was in charge of the "Big" balance dock when raising the "City of Boston" should have been in control of the balance dock that was raising the transport "Ingalls." There was an investigation made of this accident by a board of experts for the War department, but their report cannot be obtained.

# CHAPTER VIII.

HIGH WATER IN WOODEN SHIPBUILDING.—YACHT "AMERICA."—RECORD OF PROMINENT AMERICAN CLIPPER SHIPS.

HE increase in the demand on the local shipbuilders for vessels of every type, both steam and sail, from 1850 to 1855 was something phenomenal. The former date was when the California gold excitement was at its height, and the builders were unable to complete the vessels fast enough for the business of the moment, in carrying passengers and freight to the Pacific coast. The shipyards were run under high pressure, some yards working overtime, for this was a boom period in wooden shipbuilding. Many of the proprietors of the yards made large profits from the contracts they executed, and wisely invested them, while there were a few who became interested in marine speculations, particularly on the Pacific coast, that left them in a weak financial condition in the end.

There were several steam vessels that left New York for the Pacific coast at this time, a few just completed and some that had seen service, that were unfitted for such a long and tempestuous voyage. Some were certainly fortunate in ever arriving at their destination. The "New World," a beam engine boat of 216 feet long by 27 feet by 10½ feet just from the builders' hands, was sent out in February, 1850: the "Senator" that had been on the coast of Maine, and was better adapted for the voyage than some of the other vessels; the "Antelope," a comparatively new vessel that had seen service in New York bay, and the "Confidence," another New York bay vessel, neither one as large as the "New World," and never designed for such heavy weather as liable to be found on such a voyage. The greatest risk would seem to have

STEAMBOAT "RHODE ISLAND."

been taken in sending out the "Wilson G. Hunt," a small river boat of 165 feet long that had run in the upper bay, in March 1850. In six days after leaving port she encountered a gale, narrowly escaped foundering, losing her foremast, and her entire upper works being wholly wrecked by the storm. She put into St. Georges, Bermuda islands, for repairs, and subsequently proceeded on her voyage. It was not an excursion for the crew of that vessel on the voyage to San Francisco. The most unfortunate of all these vessels was the "Rhode Island," which had been on the New York and Providence route, and had been laid aside as a spare boat. She was sold to those interested in the "New World," and refitted as well as the short time would permit for the voyage. She left port January 25, 1850, and four days later encountered a violent gale. After laboring in the heavy sea for twelve hours she began to leak badly, her engine, one of the crosshead style, refused to work, while her steering gear became deranged, she was at the mercy of the waves and sank a few hours later. Twelve of the passengers and crew escaped in a small boat to a schooner that was near by at the time, but thirty-two lives were lost with the vessel. The vessel when leaving port was loaded down with coal and provisions so that her freeboard was very small for a vessel on such a voyage. The "W. J. Pease" that had been the pioneer vessel on the outside line between New York and Philadelphia, also left about the same time, and two New York tug boats, the "Goliah" and the "D. C. Pell." The "Goliah" was a large Sandy Hook tow boat but two years old, built by W. H. Webb, and was in service on the Pacific coast about ten years ago, after many changes. The record shows that the "W. J. Pease" was three months in getting well toward Cape Horn when compelled to return to Montevideo in distress in June 1850, where the vessel was repaired, but was subsequently sold and run on the Uruguay river. A mate to the "New World" named "New York" started a few months later than the former vessel, consumed about four months in getting to Rio Janeiro and there all trace of her is lost. It is believed she returned to port after first starting out, for repairs, and the second time got as far as Brazil. The "Wilson G. Hunt" seems to have been most unfortunate by detentions, for she was laid up at Montevideo for near three months for a crew, and at other ports for repairs, and the time from port to port was 322 days. The "Goliah" was 279 days on the voyage after many trials. There were several more vessels of these same types that left other Atlantic ports at the same time, and encountered the same difficulties and dangers. Several were never heard from after leaving the home port. Those that were so fortunate as to arrive at their destination were compelled to call at every principal port on the way for coal, water, provisions and repairs to the vessel, and in many cases were detained by the illness of the crew from diseases contracted in the warm climate, so it was not all pleasure that was their portion on the voyage. Very few instances are recorded of the machinery of the vessels being seriously disabled. The expenses for repairs and detention at the many ports on the voyage to San Francisco, of these light-built vessels was so great that it deterred owners from sending any more of that class of vessels under their own steam. In 1852 three or more large river steamboats were built at New York, taken apart and shipped with their machinery to San Francisco, where they were re-erected and completed for service in the waters of California.

When it became necessary during this boom period in the industry to make room for the laying of another keel, the local shipyards furnished the occasion by launching what was complete on the stocks in one-two order, and in one-two-three order, and that in all probability has never been excelled, nor ever equalled, by the shipbuilders of any nation. This it is fair to say will remain the record. And what is of additional interest, some of the vessels were so far completed that steam was on the boilers and they were ready for their trial trips as soon as they were overboard. On January 28, 1850, William H. Brown launched the "Arctic" of the Collin's line, the "New World" for the Pacific coast trade, and the "Boston" for Sanford's line on the coast of Maine. The "New World" was launched first, then the "Boston," and then the "Arctic," all put afloat within 1½ hours. This was a very skillful piece of work considering the very low temperature of the atmosphere and the liability of the tallow on the ways to chill. It was estimated that there were twenty thousand people to see the launching of these vessels, as it had been given wide advertisement for several days, and was the first time more than one vessel had been launched from one yard in a day. The "New World" was launched with her machinery all in place and ready for service, as was shown by a few revolutions of her water wheels while on the ways prior to launching. She started on her trial trip in less than one half an hour after being put overboard. This was a most novel feature of the occasion. The vessel was 216'x27'x10½' with a beam engine 40 inches by 11 feet. It was not many days before the vessel attracted attention from a different cause. There were some differences regarding the vessel between her owners, one of whom was the builder, and the vessel having been placed in the sheriff's hands, the builder desired to send her to the Pacific coast. The officers wined and dined the law officers in charge of the vessel who permitted the captain to make a "trial trip" down the bay, and when he was well into the lower bay gave them the choice of going to California with him or he would send them ashore in a small boat. They accepted the latter. It was a well planned scheme to get away from New York, for the vessel had been regularly cleared at the Custom House the day before. She made as good time as any vessel going to the Pacific Coast, being 152 days on the voyage, and was detained as little on the way by coaling, making repairs, etc., as any vessel at the time. She passed through the Straits of Magellan about the middle of April in 30 hours without stopping on the way, being six hours less time than it had been made before.* Then the steamship "Baltic" of the Collin's line of New York and Liverpool steamships was launched on March 2, 1850, with the ship "St. Louis" of 1050 tons for the New York and New Orleans trade from Jacob Bell's shipyard at Stanton and Houston streets. William H. Webb also made a double launch on June 10, 1850, when he sent overboard within a few minutes of one another the ship "Celestial" for the China trade of 1200 tons, and the steamship "Alabama" for the New York and Savannah line, both vessels going off without a mishap of any description. The next year William H. Webb added one more to the list by the triple launch on January 21, 1851, by putting overboard the steamship "Golden Gate" of 3,000 tons for the Pacific mail steamship company's service on the Pacific ocean; the ship "Isaac Bell" of 1485 tons for Livingston's line of Havre packets: and the clipper ship "Gazelle" of 1500 tons for Taylor & Merrill in the China trade on the Pacific ocean.

It was during this boom period that New York shipbuilders came to be more prominently known among the maritime nations of Europe through the building of the yacht "America." There appears to be some differences of opinion held by the early writers of the surrounding conditions prior to the building of this vessel. There is no doubt but that all who were interested in the enterprise kept the matters of detail of construction, as well as a model of the vessel from becoming public property prior to her arrival in Great Britain, and that more than probable accounts for the limited amount of information of the structure of the vessel.

---

*The same builder constructed during the same year two similar vessels to the "New World" that were launched with steam up, and that arrived on the Pacific side, named "Pacific," and "Independence."

The building of this vessel came about through a desire of a few of the members of the New York Yacht Club to have a race with the yachts of Great Britain. We must remember at this time most of the New York shipbuilders had their yards well employed in constructing merchant vessels of large dimensions, and small sailing vessels for speed, and the pilot boats and a few yachts received but small attention, as the demand for them was very limited. But one New York shipbuilder who had sufficient work on hand at his yard, still had American enterprise and love of the sport of yachting to offer George L. Schuyler of the New York Yacht Club on November 15, 1850, to build a vessel, in which he says in part: "I propose to build for you a yacht of not less than 140 tons, custom house measurement, on the following terms: The yacht to be built in the best manner, coppered, rigged, equipped with joiners' work, cabin and kitchen furniture, table furniture, water closets, etc., ready for sea. You are to designate the plan of the interior of the vessel, and select the furniture. The model, plan and rig of the vessel to be entirely at my discretion, it being understood, however, that she is to be a strong, seagoing vessel, and rigged for ocean sailing. For this vessel complete and ready for sea you are to pay me thirty thousand dollars ($30,000) upon the following conditions. * * * When the vessel is ready she is to be placed at the disposal of Hamilton Wilkes, Esq., as umpire, who after making such trials as are satisfactory to him for twenty days, shall decide whether or not she is faster than any vessel in the United States brought to compete with her. If it is decided by the umpire that she is not faster than every vessel brought against her it shall not be binding upon you to accept and pay for her at all. In addition to this if the umpire decides that she is faster than any vessel in the United States you are to have the right, instead of accepting her at that time, to send her to England, match her against anything of her size built there, and if beaten still to reject her altogether * * *" W. H. Brown."

It is clear from this letter that the builder proposed to construct the vessel, and take the risk of her acceptance upon her success in the trials with the American vessels. His offer was accepted by the yacht club and the keel of the vessel laid down in William H. Brown's yard in the last of December, 1850. There is an item of news early in January, '51, regarding this shipyard that says: "And also a yacht which her builder intends to exhibit at London during the World's Fair, as a specimen of an American yacht." The vessel was completed in May, 1851, and subjected to a few trials with Com. Stevens sloop yacht "Maria," but the schooner failed to show any superiority in speed. She proved so fast a sailor in the trials, and the builders' original offer was so great in assuming all the risk of the design, that a syndicate of several members of the New York Yacht Club was formed, composed of George L. Schuyler, Edwin A. Stevens, John C. Stevens, J. A. Hamilton and Hamilton Wilkes, who purchased the vessel for $20,000, and on June 20, 1851, the vessel was cleared from New York for London via Havre.

There have been accounts written of this vessel and naming George Steers as the builder. He no doubt made the model of the vessel for W. H. Brown as a naval architect and builder of pilot boats and yachts, and should be given credit for its design; and gave constant attention to the construction of the vessel, and yet it cannot be claimed he was the builder. This question is settled by the register of the vessel at the New York custom house, that is No. 290 of June 17, 1851, that says: "William H. Brown, only owner of the ship or vessel called the "America": That the said ship or vessel was built at the city aforesaid during the present year, 1851, as per certificate of William H. Brown, master builder, under whose direction she was built. Her length is 93' 6", her breadth

22′ 6″, her depth 9′, and she measures 170 50-95 tons. That she is a yacht schooner, has a round stern and a round tuck."

CLIPPER SHIPS.

This was the period of the greatest development of the clipper ships. This type of vessel had been built, as we have seen, by the demand for vessels in the China trade about ten years previous, but they were much smaller vessels. From the experience gained in the service of these vessels the local builders soon found the changes that were necessary in the design for the building of the larger and faster ships demanded in 1850 for the California, the China and the Australian trade. Then began the building of that large fleet of sailing vessels that gave the shipbuilders of this country such a high reputation for its clipper ships among the maritime powers of the world. There were builders outside of New York City who made a wide reputation at this time for the construction of large and fast clipper ships, notably Donald McKay, of East Boston, Mass., who had learned his trade in New York shipyards, and Currier and Townsend of Newburyport, Mass. Some of the clipper ships built at New York were the "Comet" of 1836 tons, the "Young America" of 1962 tons, the "White Squall" of 1500 tons, and the "Swordfish" of 1250 tons by William H. Webb: while Westervelt & Mackey, and Westervelt & Co. built the "Sweepstakes," the "Kathay" and the "N. B. Palmer." The "Comet" obtained the highest reputation for speed and safety during her career of the New York clippers, while the "Young America" was an exceptionally able vessel. There were several famous clipper ships built during this boom period for New York parties, or purchased by them during construction, at Eastern shipyards, notably the "Flying Cloud" and the "Dreadnought." During the height of this boom in the local shipyards there was such a scarcity of vessels that the builders of some of the Eastern shipyards constructed vessels of the clipper type on speculation, their product being eagerly taken up at good prices in many instances by New York shipping merchants. There were some of these vessels that proved in service to be ill adapted for the heavy weather encountered in the long voyage to the Pacific coast, either of faulty model or poor construction, and the expenses for repairs to such vessels were very large during almost every voyage, and there were several cargoes that were found to be seriously damaged by water on the arrival of the vessels. There was one weakness that developed with several of the larger clipper ships, and that was that they sprung their masts in a heavy blow. This was attributed to the lower end of the spars not being large enough for the heavy strain with the large spread of canvas they carried.

THE RECORD OF SOME OF THE PROMINENT CLIPPER SHIPS THAT SAILED FROM NEW YORK FROM 1841 TO 1860.

**Helena*. Built by W. H. Webb in 1841 for N. L. & G. Griswold, 135'x30' 6"x20'.

Canton to New York, 1843..............90 days
Canton to New York, April 1844........94 days
New York to Java Head, 1846...73 days 20 hours
Passed Java Head to New York, 1846..........100 days
Passed Anjier to New York, 1847..............82 days
Shanghai to New York, 1853...........102 days
Passed Java Head to New York, 1853...........82 days
Woosung to New York, 1854............97 days

**Houqua*. Built by Brown & Bell, 1844. 600 tons. A. A. Low & Co.

Canton to New York, March 1845........90 days
Canton to New York, March 1846........94 days
New York to Canton, July 1846..86 days 17 hours
Passed Java Head to Canton, July 1846..72 days 14 hours
Shanghai to New York, Feb. 1851.......88 days
Passed Anjier to New York, Feb. 1851..........72 days
Shanghai to New York, Jan. 1853......107 days

*These vessels were the first tea clippers from this country to China.

Passed Anjier to New York, Jan. 1853..........80 days
Foochow to New York, April 1854......94 days
Passed Java Head to New York, April 1854.....75 days
Foochow to New York, May 1855.......100 days

**Montauk*. Built by William H. Webb, launched April 1, 1844. 500 tons.

New York to Anjier, passed, July 1844...76 days
Whampoa to New York, March 1845.....94 days
Whampoa to New York, March 1846.....96 days
Whampoa to New York, March 1848.....93 days
New York to Sidney, Aus., August 1848..81 days

**Rainbow*. Built by Smith & Demon, launched January 22, 1845. 159'x31' 10"x18' 4". 757 tons, square stern, Howland & Aspinwall.

Sailed from New York on first voyage to Canton February 2, 1845.

Whampoa to New York, Sept. 1845.....106 days
Whampoa to New York, Sept. 1846......83 days
Whampoa to New York, March 1847.....85 days
Whampoa to New York, Feb. 1848......88 days

Left New York for Valparaiso and China on March 17, 1848, but never arrived at former port. Is thought to have been lost off Cape Horn.

**Sea Witch*. Built by Smith & Demon, 1846. Howland & Aspinwall. 907 tons.

Whampoa to New York, July 1847......83 days
Passed Anjier to New York, July 1847..........62 days
Whampoa to New York, March 1848 (?) 74 d. 14 h.
New York to San Francisco July 1850...97 days
Whampoa to New York, June 1851......98 days
New York to San Francisco Dec. 1852...100 days
Shanghai to New York, June 1853......106 days
Passed Java Head to New York, June 1853.....87 days
Valparaiso to New York, Jan. 1855......64 days

*These vessels were the first tea clippers from this country to China.

**Samuel Russell.* Built by Brown & Bell, 1847. A. A. Low & Co. 173'x34' 6"x19' 11". 957 tons.

Canton to New York, April 1848........83 days
New York to San Francisco, May 1850..108 days
Canton to New York, Jan. 1851..........88 days
Foochow to New York, Dec. 1854.......105 days
Foochow to New York, Dec. 1857......126 days
Passed Java Head to New York, Dec. 1857......78 days
Passed Cape Good Hope to New York, Dec. 1857.51 days
Foochow to New York, May 1859........95 days
Passed Anjier to New York, May 1859..........86 days
Foochow to New York, March 1860......95 days

*Oriental.* Brown & Bell, 1849. 1107 tons.

Canton to New York, April 1850........81 days
Passed Anjier to New York, April 1850.........70 days
Passed Cape Good Hope to New York, April 1850 42 days

*Surprise.* S. Hall, East Boston, 1850; 1260 tons. A. A. Low & Co.

Shanghai to New York, Jan. 1854.......97 days
Shanghai to New York, March 1855....105 days
Shanghai to New York, March 1857......85 days
Passed Anjier to New York, March 1857........70 days
Hong Kong to New York, April 1859....89 days
Passed Java Head to New York, April 1859.....76 days
Shanghai to New York, April 1860......90 days

*White Squall.* Jacob Bell, 1850. 1500 tons.

Canton to New York, March 1853.......101 days
Passed Java Head to New York, March 1853....81 days
Passed Cape Good Hope to New York March 1853 46 days
San Francisco to New York, Dec. 1853...96 days

Was so badly injured by fire at same time as the "Great Republic" as to be retired as a clipper ship; subsequently bark rigged.

*Mandarin.* Smith & Demon, 1850. 700 tons.

Shanghai to New York, May 1853.......91 days
New York to Melbourne, Dec. 1855......70 days

*These vessels were the first tea clippers from this country to China.

CLIPPER SHIP "COMET."

**In a Hurricane off Bermuda, October, 1852.**

Shanghai to New York, April 1858.....100 days
Passed Anjier to New York, April 1858..........85 days
Foochow to New York, Dec. 1859.......116 days
Passed Java Head to New York, Dec. 1859......76 days

*Comet.* William H. Webb, 1851. 229'x40'x22'.

Left New York on first voyage Oct. 1, 1851, and arrived at San Francisco January 13, 1852, 104 days.

San Francisco to Whampoa, April 1852..58 days
Whampoa to New York, Aug. 1852......96 days
Passed Anjier to New York, Aug. 1852..........72 days
New York to San Francisco, Jan. 1853..112 days
San Francisco to New York, May 1853..83 d. 18 h.
New York to San Francisco Dec. 1853...127 days
San Francisco to New York, March 1854.76 d. 7 h.
San Francisco to Cape Horn March 1854.35 d. 7 h.
Cape Horn to New York March 1854.....41 days
New York to Liverpool, May 1854.......19 days
Liverpool to Hong Kong, Sept. 1854...84 d. 16 h.
Best day's run 350 miles.
San Francisco to New York, Dec. 1857...98 days
New York to San Francisco, April 1859.112 days
San Francisco to Hong Kong, June 1859.51 days
Manila to New York, Jan. 1860.........115 days
Passed Java Head to New York, Jan. 1860......77 days
Passed Cape Good Hope to New York, Jan. 1860.41 days
Passed Java Head to New York, Jan. 1861......77 days

*Flying Cloud.* Donald McKay, 1851, 229'x41'x22', for Train & Co., of Boston, but purchased by Grinnell & Minturn of New York.

Sailed on first voyage, from New York, June 1, 1851, arrived at San Francisco August 30, 1851, 90 days 12 hours.

San Francisco to Hong Kong, Dec. 1851..47 days
Whampoa (Hong Kong) to New York, April 1852 .............................94 days
New York to San Francisco, Sept. 1852..113 days
San Francisco to Whampoa, Nov. 1852...40 days

CLIPPER SHIP "FLYING CLOUD."

Passed Honolulu from San Francisco Nov. 1852 8 d. 8½ h.
Whampoa to New York, March 1853.....97 days
New York to San Francisco Aug. 1853..105 days
New York to Cape Horn Aug. 1853......38 days
San Francisco to New York, Dec. 1853...92 days
New York to San Francisco, April 1854 89 d. 8 h.
New York to Cape Horn, April 1854.....48 days
Best day's run 360 miles.
San Francisco to Hong Kong, June 1854.37 days
Hong Kong to New York, Nov. 1854....115 days
Passed Anjier to New York, Nov. 1854...........73 days
New York to San Francisco, June 1855..110 days
New York to Cape Horn, June 1855......40 days
San Francisco to Hong Kong, Aug. 1855.46 days
Hong Kong to New York, Dec. 1855.....97 days
Passed Anjier to New York, Dec. 1855...........72 days

On her first voyage, leaving New York in June 1851, this vessel sailed for 26 days consecutively 227 2-5 knots a day. Her greatest daily performance was 374 knots: and her least daily sailing was 93 knots.

*N. B. Palmer.* Westervelt & Mackey, 1851, 1399 tons. 202″x38″x21′. A. A. Low & Co.

New York to San Francisco, Aug. 1851..107 days
Honolulu to New York, July 1854.......82 days
Manila to New York, July 1855.........99 days
Passed Anjier to New York, July 1855...........81 days
Passed Cape Good Hope to New York, July 1855.48 days
Hong Kong to New York, Jan. 1858....100 days
Passed Anjier to New York, Jan. 1858...........73 days
Shanghai to New York, Jan. 1859........82 days
Passed Anjier to New York, Jan. 1859...........64 days
Passed Cape Good Hope to New York, Jan. 1859.35 days
Canton to New York, Jan. 1860.........108 days
Passed Java Head to New York, Jan. 1860......78 days

*Trade Wind.* Jacob Bell, 1851. 2024 tons.

New York to San Francisco, Feb. 1853..103 days

San Francisco to New York, June 1853...84 days
San Francisco to New York, June 1854..89 days

*Nightingale.* Built at Portsmouth, N. H., 1851. 1300 tons.

New York to Melbourne, Aug. 1853......75 days
New York to Melbourne, Aug. 1854...76 d. 16 h.
Shanghai to New York, May 1856.......88 days
Passed Anjier to New York, May 1856..........75 days
Passed Cape Good Hope to New York, May 1856.43 days
Foochow to New York, Jan. 1860......113 days
Passed Anjier to New York, Jan. 1860..........81 days

*Swordfish.* William H. Webb, 1851. 1130 tons. 170'x36'x20'.

New York to San Francisco, Feb. 1852.90 d. 18 h.
Whampoa to New York, Jan. 1854.......97 days
Manila to New York, Feb. 1855........101 days
Manila to New York, April 1857........101 days

CLIPPER SHIP "GAZELLE."

Manila and St. Helena to New York, March 1858 ............................107 days
New York to Hong Kong, Aug. 1858.....98 days
Shanghai to New York, April 1859.....104 days
Shanghai to New York, March 1860......80 days
Passed Anjier to New York, March 1860........70 days
Passed Cape Good Hope to New York, March 1860 ............................39 days

*Gazelle.* William H. Webb, 1851. 1244 tons, 182'x38'x21'.

Whampoa to New York, April 1853.....99 days
Passed Anjier to New York, April 1853........83 days
Whampoa to New York, April 1854.....87 days
New York to San Francisco, Sept. 1854.116 days

*Invincible.* William H. Webb, 1851. 2100 tons.

London to New York, March 1853.......21 days
San Francisco to New York, Jan. 1854...90 days
Canton to New York, Oct. 1859........126 days
Passed Anjier to New York, Oct. 1859..........78 days
Liverpool to New York, Nov. 1860......16 days

*Hurricane.* Built at Hoboken, N. J., 1851. 1680 tons.

San Francisco to New York, April 1854..95 days
New York to San Francisco, Sept. 1854.100 days
New York to Cape Horn, Sept. 1854.....51 days
San Francisco to New York, Sept. 1857.105 days
San Francisco to Cape Horn, Sept. 1857.55 days

*Sovereign of the Seas.* Donald McKay, 1852. 2421 tons.

New York to San Francisco, Nov. 1852..103 days
New York to Cape Horn, Nov. 1852......51 days
Cape Horn to Equator, Nov. 1852.......33 days
The Equator to San Francisco, Nov. 1852.19 days
Honolulu to New York, May 1853.......84 days

During this voyage from Honolulu to Cape Horn of 8684 miles the trip was made in 37 days: in 26 of those days consecutively, this vessel made 6489 miles, an average of 249.6 miles per day, and on one of those days made the phenomenal run of 430 miles.

CLIPPER SHIP "SOVEREIGN OF THE SEAS."

New York to Liverpool, July 1853.....13 d. 19 h.

In 1854 this vessel was sold to parties at Hamburg, Germany.

*Flying Dutchman.* William H. Webb, 1852. 1400 tons, 190'x37'x21'.

New York to San Francisco, Jan. 1853..104 days
San Francisco to New York, May 1853...85 days
New York to San Francisco, Sept. 1853.106 days

*Contest.* D. D. Westervelt, 1852. 1100 tons.

New York to San Francisco, Feb. 1853..100 days
San Francisco to New York, May 1853.79 d. 12 h.
Tahiti Sand Islands to New York, May 1854 ................................85 days
Shanghai to New York, June 1855......99 days
Passed Java Head to New York, June 1855.....78 days
Canton to New York, March 1858......102 days

*Messenger.* Jacob Bell, 1852. 1350 tons.

Whampoa to New York, April 1853.....93 days
Passed Java Head to New York, April 1853.....61 days

*Jacob Bell.* Jacob Bell, 1852. 1440 tons.
Passed Anjier from Hong Kong to New York Dec. 1857 ..............................69 days
Passed Cape Good Hope from Hong Kong to New York, Dec. 1857...................41 days
Whampoa to New York, Jan. 1860.....104 days
Passed Anjier to New York, Jan. 1860..........77 days

*David Brown.* Roosevelt & Joyce, 1853. 1750 tons.
New York to San Francisco, March 1854.98 days
Whampoa to New York, March 1860...104 days
Passed Anjier to New York, March 1860........81 days

CLIPPER SHIP "YOUNG AMERICA."

*Young America.* W. H. Webb, 1853. 2300 tons, 235'x40'x25".
New York to San Francisco, Sept. 1853.111 days
Sandwich Islands to New York, April 1854 ............................96 days
New York to San Francisco, Oct. 1854..109 days

Manila to New York, Dec. 1855........100 days
San Francisco to New York, Dec. 1859...99 days
San Francisco to Cape Horn, Dec. 1859..44 days

*Red Jacket.* Rockland, Maine, 1853. 2434 tons.
New York to Liverpool, Jan. 1854......14 d. 8 h.
New York to Bell Buoy at Liverpool, Jan. 1854..............................13 d. 1½ h.
Liverpool to Melbourne, July 1854......69 days

*Highflyer.* Currier & Townsend, 1853. 1200 tons.
Canton to New York, April 1854........89 days
New York to Liverpool, June 1854.......24 days
Liverpool to New York, Aug. 1854......31 days
Liverpool to New York, Feb. 1855.......21 days

*Sweepstakes.* Westervelt & Mackey, 1853. 1735 tons.
New York to San Francisco, Dec. 1853...94 days
Canton to New York, July 1854........109 days
Passed Anjier to New York, July 1854..........76 days
Passed Cape Good Hope to New York, July 1854.46 days
New York to San Francisco, Feb. 1855..119 days
Shanghai to New York, March 1857....100 days
Passed Java Head to New York, March 1857....77 days

*Kathay.* Westervelt & Mackey, 1853. 1650 tons.
Canton to New York, Nov. 1854.......107 days
Passed Anjier to New York, Nov. 1854.........78 days
Shanghai to New York, Jan. 1856.......83 days
Passed Anjier to New York, Jan. 1856..........68 days
Shanghai to New York, Jan. 1857.......87 days
Passed Anjier to New York, Jan. 1857..........72 days
Amoy to New York, Feb. 1860..........93 days
Passed Anjier to New York, Feb. 1860.........74 days

*Panama.* Thomas Collyer, 1853. 1300 tons.
A fast but wet ship.
Shanghai to New York, Feb. 1853.......97 days
Passed Java Head to New York, Feb. 1853......75 days
Liverpool to New York, Feb. 1854.......22 days
Shanghai to New York, Jan. 1855....85 d. 14 h.

Passed Anjier to New York, Jan. 1855..........67 days
New York to Melbourne, July 1856.....74 d. 8 h.
Shanghai to Melbourne, March 1857.....97 days
Passed Anjier to Melbourne, March 1857.......79 days

*Ocean Telegraph.* Medford, Mass., 1854. 1600 tons.
Callao to New York, April 1855.........58 days
Honolulu to New York, June 1856......92 days
San Francisco to New York, Aug. 1859..99 days

*Great Republic.* Donald McKay, 1853.

This was the largest clipper ship built in this country, if not in the world. Her dimensions were 334½ feet by 53½ feet by 38 feet deep, having four complete decks, and fitted with four masts. These spars were re-

CLIPPER SHIP "GREAT REPUBLIC."
Fully Rigged.

markable for their dimensions, being two of 44 inches, one of 40 inches, and one of 26 inches, greatest diameter: the three largest were built of pitch pine, doweled, bolted and hooped with iron. The vessel was sent to New York to load with cargo for California, and in 29 days after her arrival, on December 27, 1853, she was badly damaged by fire from burning sparks and coal blown during a high northwest wind from a fire on shore.. The upper works of the vessel were destroyed and when rebuilt there were but three decks and three masts. A. A. Low & Bro. owned her for several years, and in 1867 she was sold, after being laid up for more than two years, to parties at Yarmouth, N. S., and name changed to "Denmark." Her record as an American vessel was now closed, as many of the prominent clipper ships of the period, in their purchase by foreign owners. In 1872 she was owned by the Merchants' Trading Company of Liverpool. She was lost during a hurricane off Bermuda while on a voyage from Rio Janeiro to St. John, N. B., on March 4, 1872. At no time was she noted for high speed. Her shortened sail area after the fire no doubt gave her less power for driving.

New York to Liverpool, March 1856............19 days
New York to San Francisco, March 1857........91 days
San Francisco to New York, March 1859........99 days

*Dreadnought.* Currier & Townsend, Newburyport, Mass., 1853, 200'x39'x26'.

Left New York on first voyage Dec. 6, 1853.

CLIPPER SHIP "DREADNOUGHT."

At Liverpool, Dec. 30, 1853..............24 days
Liverpool to New York, Feb. 1854.......19 days
New York to Liverpool, April 1854......18 days
Liverpool to New York, June 1854......26 days
New York to Liverpool, Aug. 1854......30 days
Liverpool to New York, Oct. 1854.......29 days
New York to Liverpool, Dec. 1854....13 d. 11 h.

In one day made 345 miles and in four consecutive days 1132 miles. There were few Atlantic steamships other than those of the Collin's line, and the larger ones of the Cunard line, that could beat this record at the time.

Liverpool to New York, Jan. 1855.......22 days
Liverpool to New York, Aug. 1855......27 days
New York to Liverpool, Feb. 1856.......15 days
Liverpool to New York, March 1856.....23 days
New York to Liverpool, May 1856.......16 days
Liverpool to New York, July 1856.......30 days
New York to Liverpool, Sept. 1856......21 days
Liverpool to New York, Nov. 1856......27 days
New York to Liverpool, Dec. 1856.......25 days
Liverpool to New York, Feb. 1857.......21 days

Land to land in 15 days.

New York to Liverpool, April 1857......20 days
New York to Liverpool, March 1859....13 d. 9 h.
Sandy Hook to Queenstown, March 1859 9 d. 17 h.

The log book of the "Dreadnought" containing the record of this famous voyage of March 1859 is not in existence, so far as known to the descendants of David Ogden. Captain Samuels informed the writer that on this voyage he ran the vessel to Daunt's Rock, communicated with the pilot boat on the station at the mouth of Cork harbor, and proceeded on his way to Liverpool after a very short stop. The vessel left New York harbor with a high northeast wind, but about twelve hours later this was succeeded by a high northwesterly wind on the North Atlantic coast. An examination of the reports of vessels arriving at New York from Great Britain after the "Dreadnought" sailed from New York on February 27, 1859, till the day of her call off Cork harbor show us that there were a succession of heavy westerly gales during the whole period: "experienced heavy westerly gales during whole passage:" has been 14 days west of Bermuda in heavy westerly gales: "for the first 13 days experienced nothing but high westerly gales:" "experienced very heavy weather." This favorable condition for a fast eastern passage continued to the time of the stop off Queenstown, but leaving there the "Dreadnought" encountered light head winds, and arrived at Liverpool on March 13 according to the "London Times" in 13 days. Other ship news confirmed these figures.

Some of the earlier New York built packet ships made fast voyages as well as the clipper ships.

*Natchez.*

Canton to New York, June 1843................96 days
Canton to New York, April 1844................81 days

This vessel was built by Webb & Allen in 1831: was 523 72-95 tons, $130^{3'}$x$29^{9'}$x$14^{10'}$. Custom House Register Nov. 14, 1831, for the "New Line" of packets between New York and New Orleans and was the fast sailor of the coastwise fleet of that period. She was sold to Howland & Aspinwall in 1838, who placed her in the South American trade.

*Independence.*

New York to Liverpool, 1841...........14 days 5 hours
New York to Liverpool, Feb. 1843..............18 days

*Garrick.*

New York to Liverpool, July 1844......15 days 12 hours

*Yorkshire.*

Liverpool to New York, March 1845............21 days
New York to Liverpool, Feb. 1846..............15 days

RECORD OF SOME BOSTON CLIPPER SHIPS.

*John Bertram.*

Boston to San Francisco, Oct. 1853............114 days

*Phantom.*

Boston to San Francisco, April 1853..........104 days

*Flying Fish.*

Boston to San Francisco, Jan. 1852............99 days
Boston to San Francisco, June 1853............91 days

*Northern Light.*

Boston to San Francisco, March 1852..........109 days
San Francisco to Boston, Sept. 1852...........100 days
San Francisco to Boston, May 1853.....76 days 8 hours
Boston to San Francisco, Dec. 1853............124 days
Boston to San Francisco, Sept. 1854...........125 days

*Lightning.*

Boston to Liverpool, Feb. 1854........13 days 20 hours

For ten days during a voyage of 75 days from Melbourne to Liverpool, ending in Nov. 1854 this vessel made 3722 miles. This vessel and two others, the "James Baines" and the "Champion of the Seas" were constructed by Donald McKay, of East Boston, for James Baines & Co., of Liverpool, England.

*Westward Ho.*

Boston to San Francisco, Jan. 1853...........103 days

*Star of Empire.* Donald McKay, 2050 tons, 1853.

Boston to Liverpool, May 1853.................19 days
Boston to Liverpool, Jan. 1854........14 days 15 hours

The first of the China tea clipper ships to sail by the way of Cape Horn to San Francisco was the "Helena," which left New York on March 11, 1849, with 100 passengers and freight for San Francisco, where she arrived after 163 days, and on Nov. 23 sailed from that port for Shanghai. There were previous to this date two of the tea clippers that had gone by the way of Cape Horn. The "Montauk" sailed from New York on May 26, 1848, to Sidney, Australia, in 81 days and arrived at Hong Kong on November 15. The "Sea Witch" left New York April

28, 1848, for Valparaiso where she arrived in 69 days, stopped at Callao, and sailed for Hong Kong where she arrived on December 7, 1848. The "Rainbow" sailed from New York on March 17, 1848, for Valparaiso. Her voyage was not completed. It is thought she was lost in rounding Cape Horn. These were the first of the early tea clipper ships to sail by the way of Cape Horn.

There was one ship that was in the China trade at the time of the pioneer clippers that should be mentioned. Howland & Aspinwall extended their trade with South America to China with the "Natchez" in 1842. This vessel sailed from New York June 4, 1842, for Valparaiso, where she arrived in 75 days. Left there, stopping at Callao, for Macao, China, where she arrived January 15, 1843. Left Macao for New York, where she arrived June 5. Then sailed from New York for Valparaiso June 25, where she arrived in 82 days: stopped at Callao for a cargo, and sailed for Canton, where she arrived December 17, 1843: and left Canton January 14 and arrived at New York April 20, 1844. Again sailed from New York for Canton via Valparaiso on May 20 and arrived at Canton November 20. Left Canton January 14, 1845, and arrived at New York April 3, same year. Her first voyage around the world from New York in June 1842 to June 1843 was made in one year, with two stops, while the second voyage was covered in 9 months and 26 days, including stops at three ports in discharging and receiving cargoes: and the third voyage in 10 months 14 days, including stops at two ports discharging and receiving cargoes. This was done by a New York built vessel that was constructed long before the clipper ship was called for, and for the type of vessel shows she was a fast sailor and was commanded by "a driver" without doubt. Her owners had now built the "Rainbow" for the China trade. The "Helena" had made one voyage during this period over the same route.

Those that followed via San Francisco were the

"Samuel Russell," that sailed from New York January 16, 1850, and cleared from that port on June 13 for China. The "Houqua" left New York March 15, 1850, and arrived at San Francisco in 130 days, and sailed for China from that port on September 2, 1850. The "Sea Witch" sailed from New York April 12, 1850, arrived at San Francisco in 97 days and sailed for Hong Kong on September 13. It was from the success of these vessels in their new trade, that was now assuming such large proportions, that brought into being the larger and more perfect clipper ships of that date. The "Sea Witch" and the "Samuel Russell" being the larger and the latest of these tea clippers no doubt by their superior sailing qualities over the old-time sailing ships for long voyages, had a marked influence in the design of the improved clipper ships.

It is clearly evident that the commanders of these clipper ships cannot be separated from the vessels themselves in making up the record. The names of Josiah P. Cressy, E. C. Gardner, Robert Waterman, Charles P. Low, L. McKay, Nathaniel B. Palmer, Samuel Samuels, with some others, will long be remembered as captains of the American clipper ships that had a wide reputation for high speed during that period.

### CHALLENGES TO RACE CLIPPER SHIPS.

History has handed down to us that the "Flying Cloud" was far in advance of all clipper ships of her day in making record time. She was undoubtedly a vessel having fine lines for speed, and was most ably handled in all her voyages as shown by the record: but there was one other American clipper ship of the same period that the record has shown to be her equal, and this vessel was the "Comet," a New York built vessel whose record for high speed over a long period of time is equal to any vessel of her class.

During the boom period of the clipper ship there was

considerable rivalry between the builders of this type of vessel at New York and at Boston, Mass., and so keen became the competition to produce the vessel of the highest speed and beauty of form, that all the skill of our best naval architects was brought into use. This subsequently led to challenges that were offered to test the speed of some of the clipper ships of prominence. The one case that excited most interest was that just after the "Sovereign of the Seas" made her fast voyage from Honolulu to New York, arriving on May 6, 1853, the "Comet," arriving the next day from San Francisco, having made the quickest voyage between that port and New York to that date: and though as to still further add fuel to the flame the "Flying Dutchman" arrived the next day, the 8th of May, in 85 days from San Francisco. There was the "Sovereign of the Seas" adding to the fame of the Eastern builder that credit for fast clipper ships already acquired by the high speed of the "Flying Cloud." They had not got over their shouting for what seemed to be the better model of the Boston built clipper ships, than there arrived two New York built clipper ships in phenomenal time, to upset all opinions of the knowing ones on fast sailing vessels. It was now about even with the Boston and New York built clipper ships, and this brought on a fever of speculation and banter from the opposing interests that in a few days warmed up the sporting blood in marine circles at New York and at Boston, and in a few days it was "handed out" that fifty thousand dollars was ready to be placed on the Boston built vessel in a race from New York to San Francisco in ballast or otherwise, and to sail within thirty days of each other, or together. This "chip on the shoulder" was recognized in a few days, when George Daniels the owner, and William H. Webb, the builder, of the "Young America," just completed, accepted the challenge from the owners of the "Sovereign of the Seas" for the sum of $20,000, ten thousand dollars for each, both vessels to be loaded, and to sail together or within thirty days of each other. This acceptance of the challenge was recognized by the owners of the Boston built vessel, "but the then condition of the California freight market did not offer any advantage to send the vessel to the Pacific coast," but hoped at a later date a better feeling would prevail that would enable them to place her in the San Francisco trade, and then to sail her for the stipulated amount against any ship Mr. Webb was willing to match against her. The Boston built vessel never entered the New York and San Francisco trade again.

The "Sovereign of the Seas" was registered at the Boston Custom House June 19, 1852, Donald McKay, managing owner. This register was surrendered at the New York Custom House June 18, 1853, with Andrew F. Meincke of New York as sole owner. Funck & Meincke were ship brokers at the time at 93 Wall street, New York. The next day the vessel sailed from New York for Liverpool and was engaged in the Liverpool and London, and Melbourne and China trade for some years. In May 1854 the vessel passed into the possession of J. C. Godeffroy & Son of Hamburg, Germany, who purchased her from Donald McKay, her builder.

It was some time later than the "Sovereign of the Seas" and "Young America" excitement, when those interested in the "Sweepstakes" offered to race the vessel against any of the widely-known Eastern built clippers for a distance of one thousand miles to sea, vessel for vessel. This failed to bring forth any recognition of the challenge. These two cases show how deep seated was the rivalry between some of the builders of the two cities, and what sporting blood was in the veins of our shipping interests of that period. It must be remembered we had the clipper ships of the highest speed at the time, the world over.

The prominent shipbuilders of the city and immediate vicinity, for Williamsburg and Greenpoint on the

East river, and Jersey City and Hoboken on the North river side, had begun to take over those forced out of the city by the march of public improvements and the city's expansion was in 1853, in the city proper, William H. Webb, Jacob A. Westervelt & Co., William H. Brown, William Collyer, Thomas Collyer, the one most noted for

THE "ECKFORD WEBB," OF NEW YORK.

THREE-MASTED SCHOONER "ECKFORD WEBB."

the fast river steamboats of the time, many of them narrow of beam, and cranky: Jeremiah Simonson, George Steers, the designer of the yacht "America," and builder of the Collin's steamship "Adriatic." John English, who was interested with William H. Brown in the repair work and the marine railway for several years, had this year taken the business of the new work on the withdrawal of Mr. Brown from business: Roosevelt & Joyce, successors to Brown & Bell: Smith & Demon, the oldest firm now in the business, but who retired the next year. Then in Greenpoint Eckford Webb*, E. F. Williams, E. S. Whitlock, Samuel Sneeden, Edward Lupton, Jeremiah Simonson went there in 1855. In Williamsburg there were in 1855 Lawrence & Foulks, Ariel Patterson and Thomas Stack. In Hoboken, N. J., there were Isaac C. Smith & Son and Capes & Allison. In South Brooklyn Devine Burtis, who had built some fine river steamboats.

To show the activity of the business during this boom period a few years may be cited of the tonnage put afloat for eight of those years. Launched in 1847 36,649 tons: 1848, 38,085 tons: 1849, 52,225 tons: 1850, 65,521 tons: 1851, 53,048 tons: 1852, 46,479 tons: 1853, 56,644 tons: 1854, 81,149 tons. In 1848 there were put afloat 16 steamers and 14 sailing vessels and 16 were unfinished on the stocks at the end of the year. The builders finishing the largest number of vessels this year included W. H. Webb, W. H. Brown, Westervelt & Mackey and Lawrence & Sneeden. In 1849 there were launched 3 steamships, 11 steamboats, 6 ferryboats and 24 sailing vessels, making 44 in all, and leaving 23 unfinished on the stocks. In 1850 there were put overboard 14 steamships, 16 steamboats and 33 sailing vessels, 63 in all and leaving 31 vessels unfinished on the stocks at the end of the year. The largest builders this year were Westervelt & Mackey of 10 sail and steam vessels, William H. Webb 8 steam and sail vessels: William H. Brown 9 steam vessels, 6 for Pacific coast business in which he was wholly or partly interested: and Thomas Collyer of 8 steamships and steamboats. In 1851 there were launched 17 steamships, 20 steamboats and 46 sailing vessels, 83 in all: and 23 remaining unfinished on the stocks. This was the banner year for steamboats; those building the larger number being Thomas Collyer, William Collyer, Capes & Allison, and Samuel Sneeden.

*Webb & Bell in May, 1856.

William H. Brown built this year the celebrated yacht "America." The year 1852 was not quite so lively in the shipyards, for the vessels put afloat included 41 steam vessels and 28 sail vessels, and 28 uncompleted on the stocks at the end of the year. The builders of the largest number of vessels were Westervelt & Co., William H. Webb and Jeremiah Simonson. In 1853 there were launched in New York and immediate vicinity 37 steam vessels and 43 sailing vessels, the builders of the largest number this year being W. H. Webb, Westervelt & Co., Perrine, Patterson & Stack, and Isaac C. Smith & Son. In 1854 there were launched 43 steam vessels and 68 sailing vessels, in all 111 vessels, and there were on the stocks at the end of the year 18 sailing vessels and 4 steam vessels that were unfinished. There were 31 more vessels launched in 1854 than the year previous. In 1855 there was a falling off in the number of vessels put afloat, for there were but 38 sailing vessels and 13 steam vessels launched, and 21 left on the stocks for completion. William H. Webb, Westervelt & Co. and Jeremiah Simonson were the builders of the largest number of vessels this year. During the next year there were launched 12 steam vessels and 43 sailing vessels, the builders of the largest number being William H. Webb, George Steers & Co., Webb & Bell, and William Collyer.

In 1847 there were about 2400 ship carpenters, ship-joiners, caulkers and sawyers employed in the shipyards of the city and vicinity, and by 1850 this number of employees had been increased about 10 per cent. The prevailing rate of wages had been very steadily maintained at $2.00 for 10 hours a day. About 1853 began the building of steamers for China waters that assumed such large proportions in a few years. The marine railway that was located at the foot of East 10th street since 1826 was removed in 1855 to Hunters Point, now known as Long Island City.

The machine bending of ship timber was brought

into use from experiments made in bending timber of the sizes adopted for furniture, and the principle was applied to timber of larger size, until at length live oak 11"x13" by 10 feet long, sawed, squared and straight, had been bent to the required crook of a second futtock, by the principle of end pressure. It was not thought possible when the American Bending Company was formed in 1853 to do more than bend futtocks of a very moderate size. In the same year a pair of bent futtocks was put in the steamer "Ocean Bird": this was the proposed "6 day steamer" built by J. W. Griffith. In 1856 a full set of bent hanging knees was put into the bark "Lexington" of 412 tons, built by Edward F. Williams at Greenpoint, L. I., and in the same year a set of bent knees for both decks of the bark, "Jane Daggett" of 840 tons built by Webb & Bell. In 1858 the steam sloop of war "Pawnee" was fitted with sixty machine bent timbers from twenty to twenty-four feet in length, that were the largest that had been used to that time, and in the same year the ship "Richard S. Ely" of 1200 tons, built at Boston, Mass., was fitted with bent hanging knees. Machine bent knees continued to be occasionally used, but it was not until 1869-70 that a ship with bent frames and knees was built by John W. Griffiths, one of the original promoters at East Boston, Mass. This vessel was named "New Era," was of 1146 tons and proved to be in service a very strong built vessel, dry, and a good carrier and obtained high rates for freight, with low rates of insurance. This was about the last of the machine bent knees to any extent. Wooden shipbuilding now fell off, and there being no increase of the business, it gradually fell by the wayside.

The "Dry Dock" section of the city was the locality between Houston and 12th streets, and from the river as far inland as Avenue C, and within these boundaries were many shops and factories that catered more or less to the fitting and furnishing of vessels. They each had a greater or lesser number of employees who knew no other time monitor than the mechanics' bell, and during the boom period it was a sight to behold the hundreds that came in haste—they did not walk—from the yards and shops on their way to their homes, that were mainly in the vicinity, at the evening tap of the bell. A stranger would be surprised where they all came from in such a short time. It was not the shipyards alone that furnished this vast throng of mechanics, but the four or more marine engine works, and the smaller factories that added their quota to the small army.

In 1855 some of the works of the allied trades to shipbuilding in the locality of the dry dock included the Novelty Iron Works: Secor Iron Works: Dry Dock Iron Works, J. S. Underhill: John Powers & Co., machinists: Youngs & Cutter, ship joiners: Richard Squires, painter: Brooks & Cummings, coppersmiths: John A. Seamen, ship chandler: Morgan Iron Works: Lewis Raymond, boat builder: Neptune Iron Works; Boardman, Holbrook & Epps: John E. Hoffmire, ship joiner: Andrew Reed, and Rodney S. Sugar, shipwrights: David J. Taff, spars:* Horton & Arnold, and Watts & Sheffield, edge tools, and John Tiebout, hardware: Charles Simonson, ship joiner: Cornelius Winant, spar maker.*

There were several shipyards at this time on the opposite side of the river that were also largely engaged in construction of vessels and employed many skilled mechanics, and others, in the prosecution of their work, and who knew the tone of the old mechanics bell from all other bells, and obeyed its call to duty.

---

*There were two other spar makers at the time located at Corlears Hook, George Thorburn in Cherry street, and Abram Denike & Co., in Water street.

# CHAPTER IX.

## DECLINE OF WOODEN SHIPBUILDING.

N the latter part of 1854 were seen the first signs of the effect of the high pressure under which the business of wooden shipbuilding had been operated in New York City for several years. New yards had been opened, and in some cases these builders having limited capital to carry out their contracts, that they had taken in competition with the older and more experienced builders, two or three of them were forced to suspend business, and in some few cases their effects were sold by the sheriff. This occasioned a season of depression in the local business that had not been felt in many years. The prevailing high prices of material and rate of wages contributed a large share to the result; or rather the attempt to construct a vessel for less than its cost, has never proved a profitable adventure. Timber that formerly cost $28 M. feet, now cost $36 to $40. Southern pine plank $24 M. feet, Western p. plank $32. Oak ship plank $35 to $40. Hackmatack knees 7 inches, 40 cents per inch. Refined iron advanced from $40 to $85 a ton. Copper from 25 cents to 30 cents per pound; and labor from $2 and $2.50 to $3 per day, and even at the latter rate of wages the skilled labor refused to be steadily employed. With these conditions surrounding the builders, and the fact of many contracts being taken subject to a time penalty, it is not strange that some of them were forced to suspend business. These same conditions continued during the next year and the want of a more agreeable feeling between employer and employee became manifest, and the exorbitant demand of the skilled labor, as it then appeared, caused a want of harmony that lead to much ill feeling between those interested. The unfulfilled contracts had to be completed, and the builders were at the mercy of the mechanics for the time being, so they were compelled to submit to their demands for an increase of wages. This state of things enabled the skilled labor to earn in four days in many cases as much as was deemed by him a fair week's wages, and many under the circumstances refused to remain at work steadily for the entire week of six working days. One of the ship carpenters who was employed at this period told the writer recently, that he was making so much money at that time from the high rate of wages paid to ship carpenters that he was compelled to take one or two days vacation each week to keep the accumulated capital from becoming a burden. He says he sees his error now. It was early in 1856 when several of the contracts had been completed, and new contracts for vessels not being made, that the effect of this agitation began to be seen and felt, by those least able to bear it. The good times in the New York shipyards of 1848 to 1854 never returned, except for periods during the Civil war.

There were other reasons for the depression and decline of shipbuilding at the period under review. The steamboat law of 1852, that was not put into practical effect until late in 1853, had the effect of forcing capital to seek other investments than marine property, as there was not that freedom of individual control and operation of steam vessels that had existed prior to the enactment of that law: this affected more especially our river and sound lines of vessels. Our capitalists were now engaged in the development of our steam railroads.

By 1856 the fever of the California gold excitement had passed off, and all the vessels that were required in that trade, on both the Atlantic and Pacific sides of the continent, were now in strong hands financially, the speculating contractor having served his day in that quarter.

What added a further depressing influence to the extension of our merchant marine was the agitation of the withdrawal of the mail subsidy from the Collin's line of steamers by Congress, that was carried into effect shortly after. The determined and patriotic exertions of the British shipping interests to help their country's cause at this time, was in a directly opposite course to that of our Congress, which was accomplishing everything it could through legislative action to hamper and annoy our shipowners and force them into bankruptcy: this is shown by the proceedings of Congress. But what had a most lasting effect upon our shipbuilding industry was the failure of our shipowners to see at that early day that the iron hull vessel was to replace the wooden hull, and that at once. Great Britain had been for several years building iron hull steam vessels, though the first transatlantic iron hull steamship of a permanent line had not been put in service until 1850, when the propeller "City of Glasgow" was operated by the Inman line, and a few years later the Cunard line had for a time two iron hull screw steamers, but their first iron hull paddle wheel steamship "Persia" was not built until 1856. The Hamburg-American Packet Company put in service to this country iron hull steam vessels in 1855, and the North German Lloyds Company operated their first iron hull steam vessel to this country in 1857. The Anchor line came in a little later. It is thus seen that Great Britain had very generally laid aside the wooden hull for the iron hull steam vessel, at the time we were building such fleets of large wooden hull steamships and even large sailing vessels, and even later, there were several large wooden hull steamships built for the European and coastwise trade, while the foreign companies were adding new vessels built of iron. So wedded to the wooden hull had become our shipbuilders and shipowners, for it must be remembered that the builder was in some instances interested in a transportation company for whom he built vessels, and the owners in such cases likely to be influenced by the professional opinion of the builder as to the design and construction of a vessel, that the latter found it hard to break away from his early business education that wooden hulls would rule for ages. He did not let go until forced by surrounding conditions. The building of iron hull vessels in this country up to 1850, outside of those built for experiments, consisted of 21 steam vessels for inland waters of 175 feet in length and less, two naval vessels, eight steam revenue cutters of an average length of 160 feet, one coastwise propeller 120 feet long, and two fine river passenger steamboats of about 240 feet in length. There were at this period but three iron shipbuilding yards in this country, Harlan & Hollingsworth Company at Wilmington, Del.; Reanie Neafie & Co., at Philadelphia, Pa., and Pusey & Jones Company, Wilmington, Del., besides Robert L. Stevens' works at Hoboken, N. J. This shows that some experience had been acquired by our constructors in the building of iron hull vessels up to 1850, and with an increase of facilities for production, they would be able to meet all demands for domestic vessels of larger dimensions. Our iron rolling mills were able to furnish the material for construction, and our tool makers the necessary tools for working the heavier material, and our engineers, engines of greater power, as the first year of the Civil War proved in the refitting of several plants for building iron vessels. In proof of this there were before 1860 five coastwise iron hull steam vessels, all constructed on the Atlantic coast, four about 220 feet long and one 142 feet in length, and vessels that were operated for many years. It is true, that there had not been to this time any effort made to build larger vessels of iron hull for the foreign trade for the simple reason that the treatment received by the Collin's line company, as well as other American steamship companies in the European trade, by the Congress of the United States, was anything but encouraging to the steamship owners at the time to invest their capital in a more modern type of vessel. Cornelius Vanderbilt had built the first and largest iron hull steamship prior to the Civil War in this country, after which our shipbuilders were engaged in doing their part for the nation's preservation. The Civil War did not cause the decline of our merchant marine: it had started on the downward course toward extinction by 1861, but the Rebellion was only a cause that hastened its fall.

During the Civil War there was an abundance of work at the local shipyards in the alterations made on vessels purchased by the Navy department for the blockading fleet, and those for special service of the department. Later there were many steam vessels built for private parties that were purchased by the government

for the transport service. The Navy department had six screw gunboats of 507 tons each built in 1861 by Webb & Bell, John English, Thomas Stack, J. A. Westervelt & Co., Jeremiah Simonson and C. & R. Poillon. The next year there were five wooden hull double enders built of 974 tons each, for the blockading fleet by J. A. & D. Westervelt, Thomas Stack, Jeremiah Simonson, Edward Lupton and F. Z. Tucker at Devine Burtis' old yard, at the local shipyards. The government work and that for the merchant service kept the yards well employed during the war times, though there were not so many builders as a decade before.

During this war period our wooden hull shipbuilders had not yet fully learned that iron hull propellers were the coming type of ocean carriers, for there were built ten of those large beam engine side wheel steamships for the Pacific Mail Steamship Company over 300 feet long each, and a little later there were built three side wheelers by Henry Steers for the Nicaragua Transit Company of near 300 feet in length each; and two propellers were built by Newburyport, Mass., builders for a Boston Company, for a Boston and Liverpool line, of about the same dimensions, all these vessels having wooden hulls. This was about the last of that type of vessel.

While there were several vessels under construction at the local shipyards during 1866, in the spring of the next year there was but one vessel under construction in the shipyards of New York and vicinity. Take this as a contrast with the month of September, 1863, when there were thirty-two large vessels, each of a thousand tons or over, in process of construction in the shipyards of New York. This was during the period when they were building merchant vessels for special service, and the government being in want of steam vessels for transport service principally, made contracts to purchase the vessels on completion long before they were finished. There is no doubt some of the vessels were put under contract, knowing the pressing necessity of the government at the time. The depression in the industry in 1866 was mainly caused by the government throwing on the market by public auction a large number of vessels they had no further use for at the close of the War of the Rebellion, mainly those that had been in the blockading fleet, or in the transport service, and were adapted for the coastwise merchant service or the river passenger trade.

There were sold by the Navy department at Boston, Mass., New York City, Philadelphia, Pa., and Washington, D. C., just after the close of the Rebellion 219 steam vessels that had been in the blockade squadron, and same as transports of supplies to the naval vessels and stations on the Atlantic coast. About the same time there were sold at public sale also, by the quartermaster's bureau of the War department, 140 steam vessels that had been used during the military operations, for the transportation of troops and supplies on the Atlantic coast and in the Gulf of Mexico. The larger number of the vessels in the service of the War department were of the better class of our sound and river passenger steamboats, though there were some pretty ancient vessels purchased, or taken under contract. There were comparatively few vessels fitted for the coastwise trade as the Navy department had most of them.

The ship carpenters, ship joiners and caulkers, and other employees of the New York shipyards can lay claim to having been the first labor organizations to throw down the gauntlet, or strike, for an eight hour day in this country. They seem to have been the advance guard in both of the labor movements for a reduction in the hours of labor in this country. The labor agitators had been for some time again at work in this country to show to the skilled mechanics the value of their services in labor's interest. They had been agitating and looking for trouble, but the mechanic had been too busily employed at a high rate of wages to be attracted to any labor reform movement. After being worked upon for some time by these outside interests, that were using the shipyard employees for their own selfish purposes, the shipyard employees struck for an eight-hour day on April 2, 1866. No complaint was made of the rate of wages paid at the time. There were about five thousand men engaged in the strike, that had extended to some trades allied to shipbuilding. The strike was continued for ten weeks, when the labor organization agreed to rescind the resolution made by them, calling on the employers to reduce the hours of labor from ten to eight hours. They shortly after went back to work, such as could find employment at the old hours. This was a bitter contest while it lasted, and was at times accompanied with violence on the part of the strikers or their sympathizers. The loss of this strike was a great disappointment to the local labor interests, especially as great hopes for a general eight-hour day had been laid on the success of this strike. A great deal of repair business in the shipyards that always came to New York was at this time sent to other cities to be done, and this trade never returned. The skilled labor at the shipyards was now receiving $4 to $4.50 per day. The greater number of the better class of the skilled laborers in the shipyards were opposed to this movement, seeing the fine work under the surface, and that it was manipulated to other interests than those of the laborers in the shipyards. This was an ill-advised move for the shipyard employees, that most of them found out very soon to their great disadvantage. There were many worthy men taking no hand in the strike, that had to suffer the consequences with those that were active in the movement, and of less ability at their trade.

The shipbuilders in 1866 in New York City and vicinity were Westervelt & Company, William H. Webb, Jeremiah Simonson, John English & Son, Waterbury & Joyce, C. & R. Poillon, Webb & Bell, Samuel Sneeden, Lawrence & Foulks, Thomas Stack, Edward F. Williams and Henry Steers. Wages fell off on account of less demand for the skilled labor, and by the latter part of 1869 had fallen to $3.25 per day. Material was quoted at this time, hemp for caulking 12 cents, copper 34 cents per pound, hackmatack knees $2.75, oak timber $60, white pine $45.

It must not be supposed that all the wooden hull shipbuilders in New York and the immediate vicinity closed up business about 1868. It appears by looking over a list of the more prominent builders of this period that those who retired at about the former date were builders who constructed steamships and the larger sailing vessels, those engaged in the ocean trade to foreign countries, while those who were more prominently known as constructors of steam vessels for sound service and the inland waters still retained their shipyards, and had

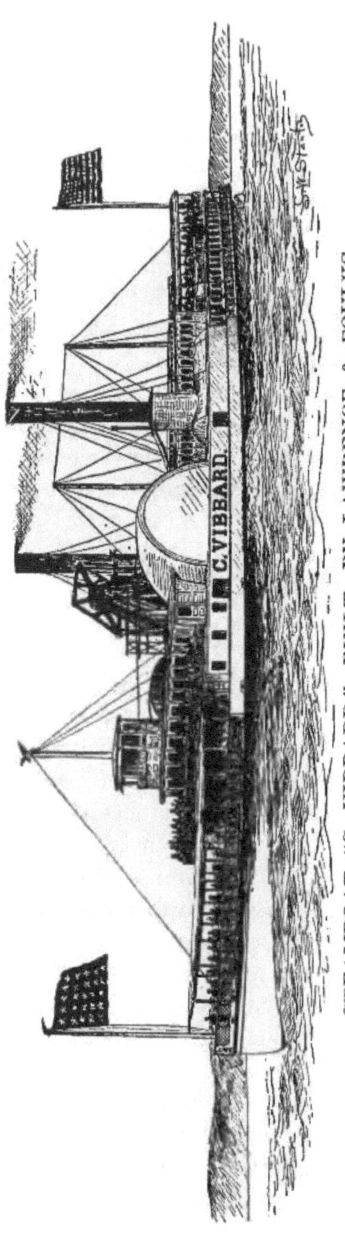


STEAMBOAT "C. VIBBARD," BUILT BY LAWRENCE & FOULKS.

more or less new vessels to construct for some years, with repair work for their old patrons. It will be said that some builders were largely interested in the transportation companies that gave them a preference in much new work, as well as the repair work that was the more profitable, whereby they continued later in the business. That will be granted. It was the case with some of our shipbuilders during the boom period; they became financially interested in some of the American transportation companies, controlled all the new work and repairs of the vessels for the companies, and amassed large fortunes that were wisely invested, so that when the wooden hull vessel had mainly passed by they were in a position to fall back on their savings, and some became actively interested in other lines of business.

The only builders left in 1870 in New York City and vicinity were: William H. Webb in the city proper, and Lawrence & Foulks, Thomas Stack, Webb & Bell, and John English & Son, in the vicinity having any vessels under construction. The William H. Webb yard was idle. In the last two years Waterbury & Joyce, Samuel Sneeden, Jeremiah Simonson, Edward F. Williams and Elisha S. Whitlock had gone out of the business of shipbuilding. Jacob A. Westervelt was dock commissioner of New York City from 1870 to the time of his death in January, 1879. Samuel Sneeden had a yard on the Hudson river opposite upper part of the city, where he built a few vessels. Jeremiah Simonson was a U. S. steamboat inspector for a few years from 1876. George Bell and Eckford Webb became interested in paint manufacturing in Williamsburg. Herbert Lawrence retained his old office at Greenpoint to the time of his death about four years ago, and the successors of John English & Son retain their old office, and construct joiner work for vessels in which they are interested.

The last new work of any moment completed by some of the wooden hull builders in New York would include William H. Webb in building the ship "Charles H. Marshall" of 1600 tons in 1869: Jeremiah Simonson in 1866 in building four side wheel steamboats, the "Grampus," "Manatus," "Walrus" and "Nautilus"; the two first named were subsequently the "Stonington" and the "Narragansett" of the New York and Providence Company. Thomas Stack in building the propeller "Fern" in 1872 for the Light House Board. Herbert Lawrence, Lawrence & Foulks, steamboat "Albertina" in 1882 for the Red Bank line, and in 1892 the steam yacht, side-wheel "Clermont" for Com. Alfred Van Santvoord of the New York and Albany day line. This was the most skillful designer of our high-speed river steamboats of the period. Webb & Bell, of the ferryboat "Winona" in 1869 for the Union ferry company, of Brooklyn, N. Y. In 1871 they constructed the caissons for the Brooklyn bridge. C. & R. Poillon in building the auxiliary yacht "Oonas" in 1901 for W. H. Alley of Chicago, Ill. John English & Son the steamboat "Adirondack" in 1896 for the People's line between New York and Albany. Devine Burtis, Jr., the steamboat "General Slocum" in 1891. Westervelt & Son in 1865 building the steamships "Niagara" and the "Saratoga" for the New York and Richmond line; and in 1866 the "Foong Shuey" or "Plymouth Rock" for China waters. Henry Steers at Greenpoint in 1877 the "Massachusetts" for the New York and Providence line. Thomas Collyer & Co. in 1863 the steamboat "Thomas Collyer," now known as "Sam Sloan." Joseph Van Dusen, foot East 18th street, yacht "Fleetwing" in 1866. Samuel H. Pine in 1893, steamboat "Mary Patten" for the New York and Shrewsbury river line.

The last "square riggers" built in New York or the immediate vicinity were two half-brigs by C. & R. Poillon at foot Bridge street, Brooklyn. The first was the "Ruby" of 233 tons completed in December, 1873, and the "Garnet" of 237 tons, built in 1877, both for D. Trowbridge & Co., of New Haven, Conn. The last record there is of the former is in 1892, and of the latter in 1899. The last ship built at New York was by William H. Webb in 1869, the "Charles H. Marshall" of 1600 tons. The last bark was the "James A. Borland" of 600 tons, built by William H. Webb in 1868. This vessel was in service on the Pacific Coast in 1897.

Other parties now came forward with more advanced ideas of the needs of the marine interests of the country, and with propositions to put it on a more stable footing, but it was not carried out until after a most determined fight against strong odds. All the interests opposed to the advancement and strengthening of the American marine were arrayed against them. Now came the real opening of our iron shipbuilding. Our wooden hull shipbuilders and shipowners had maintained a most determined opposition to any change and paid a high price for holding fast to a principle, long after it was seen by others to be lost. But they had at last to succumb to the inevitable. As iron forced out the wooden hull vessel, so steel has replaced the iron hull vessel. There were many of the wooden hull steam vessels that were purchased at public auction from the United States government at the close of the Civil War, and placed on coastwise lines, as well as on inland waters that were no longer of service by 1873 on account of their being constructed in many instances of unseasoned timber, and the want of proper care during their military service. The demand for new vessels to take the places of these unfit vessels, gave the iron shipbuilders in this country an opportunity to secure orders for iron hull vessels, though they were few at first, as the country was then suffering from a business depression that lasted nearly five years.

There is at this time not one of the old wooden shipbuilders or their successors who have a shipyard at New York for building a wooden hull vessel, or for making extensive repairs to such a vessel. There are a few small yards in the vicinity of New York where wooden car floats, small sail vessels, scows and barges are constructed and repaired for local service. The repair work on the larger vessels is now carried on mainly by the dry dock companies who have every facility for docking a vessel and making extensive repairs where such becomes necessary. There are three or more iron shipbuilding yards where there are dry docks and where new and repair work are executed. There is in New York and the immediate vicinity at this time (1909) 5 marine railways, 32 floating docks, 200 feet long and under, 2 over 200 feet long, 4 sectional over 200 feet long, 8 sectional over 300 feet long, one balance dock over 300 feet long, and 5 balance docks under 300 feet long each.

There is nothing left at this day to show where the shipyards in New York during the period of their greatest prosperity were located. Even the old mechanics bell has been removed from its last home of activity to a place of storage at Webb's Academy and Home for Shipbuilders. The "Big" balance dock is about the only material evidence left to us of the days of the wooden shipbuilders' activity. Last, but not least, are the very few, not more than forty in all, and this number decreasing very rapidly, of the old employees of the New York shipyards, a few living in New York and the immediate vicinity, and the remainder at the Webb Home as guests of the late William H. Webb.

Thus has passed forever, the old time shipyards of New York, that kept pace with the industrial progress of the United States for more than fifty years.

# INDEX.

Zeitfracht Medien GmbH
Ferdinand-Jühlke-Straße 7
99095 Erfurt, Deutschland
produktsicherheit@kolibri360.de